CONTENTS

KT-484-262

A note for teachers

This book contains a variety of suggested food technology projects. They range in complexity from topics about single foods to projects where students are required to apply the design process to broader situations in the food industry.

▸ Most projects include a practical element, which in most cases can be adapted to suit the constraints of time and available facilities.

▸ Guidelines for research are provided, but these are by no means exhaustive, so students need to be encouraged to develop their own research techniques.

▸ The first few projects provide a fairly detailed framework for students to follow, so that they understand how to approach and undertake future projects.

▸ Some projects give information about the topic, to set the scene for students so that they have a starting point on which to base their own research.

▸ Where appropriate, more than one brief is given, in order to show a variety of ways of approaching a topic.

Weights and measures
Common weights for measuring foods: 5 g, 10 g, 20 g, 50 g, 100 g, 150 g, 250 g, 500 g, 1k g
Common measures for liquids: 25 ml, 50 ml, 75 ml, 100 ml, 250 ml (quarter of a litre), 500 ml (half a litre), 1 litre

Food
Technology

OXFORD

OXFORD
UNIVERSITY PRESS

Great Clarendon Street, Oxford OX2 6DP

Oxford University Press is a department of the University of Oxford.
It furthers the University's objective of excellence in research,
scholarship, and education by publishing worldwide in

Oxford New York

Auckland Bangkok Buenos Aires Cape Town Chennai
Dar es Salaam Delhi Hong Kong Istanbul Karachi Kolkata
Kuala Lumpur Madrid Melbourne Mexico City Mumbai Nairobi
São Paulo Shanghai Taipei Tokyo Toronto

Oxford is a registered trade mark of Oxford University Press
in the UK and in certain other countries

British Library Cataloguing in Publication Data

Data available

ISBN 0 19 832819 2

10 9 8 7 6 5 4 3 2

Printed in Spain by Edelvives, Zaragoza

Acknowledgements

The publishers would like to thank the following for permission to
reproduce photographs:

Front cover: Corbis Stockmarket (main picture), Stockbyte and Corel (cut
outs); Title page: Corbis Stockmarket; p5: Telegraph Colour
Library/Denis Boissavy; p6: Telegraph Colour Library/Simon Witmore
(bottom left), Anthony Blake Picture Library/Rosenfeld Images (bottom
centre), Anthony Blake Picture Library/Tim MacPherson (bottom right);
p8: Anthony Blake Picture Library/Maximilian (bottom): Oxford
University Press (top); p10: Anthony Blake Picture Library/Maximilian
(top), Oxford University Press (bottom); p11: Oxford University Press;
p14: Stockbyte (left 1, 2, 3, 5, 6,), Corel (left 4); p15: Anthony Blake Picture
Library/Maximilian; p17: Corel (left 1, 4), Anthony Blake Picture
Library/Tim Hill (left 2), Anthony Blake Picture Library (left 3),
Stockbyte (bottom centre); p19: Corbis/Mark Gibson (top); p21: Anthony
Blake Picture Library/Gerrit Buntrock; p22: Robert Harding Picture
Library (top and bottom); p23: Robert Harding Picture Library; p24:
Corbis/Gehe Company (top left), Oxford University Press (top right); p26:
Corbis/Bob Rowan (left 1), Corel (left 2, 3, 4, 6), Stockbyte (left 5); p27:
Stockbyte (left 1), Corel (left 2, 3, 4); p28: Anthony Blake Picture
Library/Brian Limage (centre); p29: Anthony Blake Picture
Library/Philip Wilkins; p32: Holt Studios/Nigel Cattlin; p34: Science
Photo Library/David Scharf (left and right), Science Photo
Library/Microfield Scientific (middle); p36: Oxford University Press; p38:
Robert Harding/Paul Van Riel; p49: Corbis/Bettmann (top), Corbis/Liba
Taylor (bottom); p50: Robert Harding Picture Library/Robert French;
p51: Anthony Blake Picture Library/Graham Salter (top), Anthony
Blake/Phototeque Culinaire (bottom right), Mary Evans Picture Library
(bottom left); p52: Robert Harding/Gavin Hellier (top), Anthony Blake
Picture Library/Graham Kirk (bottom left), Anthony Blake Picture
Library/Stephen Read (bottom right), Stockbyte (inset); p54: Corel; p55:
Allsport (left), T O'Keefe (right); p58: Robert Harding Picture
Library/Westerman (top), Corbis/Tempsport (bottom left), Oxford
University Press (bottom right); p62: Corbis/Paul A Souders; p63: Oxford
University Press; p64: Holt Studios/Nigel Cattlin (top); p66: Anthony
Blake Picture Library/Maximilian (bottom left), Anthony Blake Picture
Library/Maximilian (bottom right); p67: Anthony Blake Picture
Library/Premium; p68: Oxford University Press; p74: Robert Harding
Picture Library/Rob Cousins (left); p77: Anthony Blake Picture
Library/Maximilian (right); p78: Robert Harding Picture Library/Scott
Barrow (left), Robert Harding Picture Library/Mark Mawson (right); p79:
Oxford University Press; p80: Robert Harding Picture Library; p84:
Anthony Blake Picture Library/Maximilian (top), Anthony Blake
Picture Library/Tony Robins (bottom); p85: Anthony Blake Picture
Library/Maximilian; p86: Oxford University Press (both); p89: Courtesy
of Keith Hosking, Withey Limited (right); p90: Holt Studios/Nigel Cattlin
(left), Anthony Blake Picture Library/Joy Skipper (right); p92: Oxford
University Press; p94: Oxford University Press; p98: Corel (all); p99:
Oxford University Press; p104: Anthony Blake Picture Library/James
Murphy; p105: Corbis/Bob Rowan; p108: Anthony Blake Picture
Library/Joy Skipper (bottom); p109: Anthony Blake Picture
Library/Kieran Scott (left), Oxford University Press (right); p110: Oxford
University Press (left); p113: Oxford University Press; p116: Hulton
Archive (left), Oxford University Press (right); p120: Anthony Blake
Picture Library/Rosenfeld Images; p121: Anthony Blake Picture
Library/Maximilian; p124: Oxford University Press (right)

Special thanks to J Sainsbury plc

Additional photography by Rob Judges, Martin Sookias and David Tolley

Illustrations by Martin Aston and David Russell

A note for students

Throughout this book there are ideas for projects that let you explore food technology in greater depth. The first ones show you step-by-step how to produce a successful project. Some of the topics are more detailed than others, and your teacher will help you decide which ones to try.

Whichever project you try, remember these points:

▶ try to present your written and practical work in a neat, clear and interesting way

▶ when finding out about a topic, ask questions, look, listen, read and think about what you find out

▶ when someone reads your project, they should be able to learn something from it

▶ enjoy yourself!

The Internet is a useful source of information for projects.

Introduction

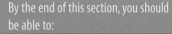

What is food technology?

By the end of this section, you should be able to:
- Understand what food technology means.
- Identify the different parts of the food industry.
- Identify some of the effects that the food industry has on people and places.

Food technology is the study of how different foods can be used and made into food products.

Before they are ready to be sold in the shops, food products go through a series of tests and studies to make sure that they are:
- safe to eat
- good to eat
- easy to use
- well packaged
- a reasonable price

In this book we will be finding out how new food products are designed and made and how the food industry provides us with our daily food.

The food industry

The food industry is very large and includes:
- food producers (people who grow food)
- food manufacturers (people who make food products)
- food distributors (people who supply foods to shops, restaurants, schools, hospitals)
- food retailers (people who sell food)
- food providers (people who cook and sell food in restaurants, canteens, etc.)

Food producers grow food.

Food manufacturers make food products.

Food providers cook and sell food.

People have been growing, making and selling food to other people for hundreds of years, but it was during the 20th century that the food industry became very large. Why did this happen? What were the consequences of the growth of the food industry?

Why did this happen?	What were the consequences?	
governments encouraged farmers to grow more food	▶ many foods became cheaper and easier for people to buy	➤ environmental damage big changes to the countryside (loss of hedgerows, ponds and woodland and other natural habitats for wildlife)
transport by land, sea and air became easier	▶ people travelled abroad and tried food from other countries	➤ foreign restaurants opened foreign foods sold in shops
	▶ food grown in one country could be sent to another country and arrive there in good condition	➤ some foods, e.g. strawberries, could be eaten all year round
	▶ people used cars to buy their food from supermarkets	➤ air pollution and less exercise for people
growth of technology	▶ food could be grown and harvested on a large scale using machinery	➤ fewer people needed to work on farms
	▶ new food products were invented, e.g. low-fat spreads, breakfast cereals, instant puddings	➤ people had more choice
	▶ new ways of preventing food from 'going off' (preserving food) could be used, e.g. UHT milk, frozen foods, vacuum packaging	➤ food shopping needed to be done less often

QUESTIONS

1 List the food producers, manufacturers, distributors, retailers and providers in the local area (a telephone directory will help you).

2 Write down why you think some of the food shops, restaurants, factories or warehouses in your area have been built in certain places. For example, are they:
   ▶ near a motorway or airport?
   ▶ in a town centre near offices and other shops?
   ▶ in a housing estate?
   ▶ near a river or the sea?

3 What effects do you think the following might have on the local environment:
   a) an out-of-town supermarket
   b) a high-street take-away burger bar
   c) a meat pie factory near a housing estate
   d) a large wheat field growing by a river?

The design process

By the end of this section, you should be able to:
- Understand what the design process is.
- Identify the different stages of the design process.
- Explain why it is important for a food manufacturer to work through the design process when producing a new food product.

The series of tests and studies that all new food products go through before they are ready to be sold is called the **design process**. All new products, including cars, toys, kitchen equipment, medicines, and so on, go through a similar process.

There are several stages in the design process for food products. A food manufacturer may repeat some stages when designing a new food product.

Stage 1: Is a new product needed?

This can be called 'establishing a need'. There are several reasons why a manufacturer might think a new product is needed:
- a customer might ask for a new product
- research (finding out) may suggest a new product is needed
- there may be a problem with an existing product, so it needs to be changed
- there may be changes in the types of food people want to eat, for example, they may want foods with less fat or sugar in them

A market researcher conducts an interview with a member of the public.

To find out more about whether a new product is needed, the manufacturer might carry out some **market research**. Market researchers will find out about the people who they think might buy the product and about similar products that are available:

About people	About food products
- why people buy certain food products - how people live (their lifestyle) - how much money they spend on food - how much cooking they do at home - how often they eat out in restaurants - how much notice they take of food issues, e.g. healthy eating advice, where and how food is grown, food advertising, damage to the environment, animal welfare	- how they are made - what they look, smell, taste and feel like - what happens when they are frozen, cooked in a microwave oven, baked, and so on - how well their packaging works (is it easy to read and open, does it protect the food?) - are they suitable for vegetarians, people with allergies, babies, and so on? - do they meet people's needs, e.g. are they easy to prepare and use and healthy, are the portion sizes suitable?

Testers carry out sensory analysis.

To find out such information, market researchers use a variety of methods, for example:
- **Interviews** with people, in which they are asked questions from a survey or questionnaire. This might be done through the post, on the telephone, or face to face in the street.
- **Sampling** similar food products to the one being designed, and giving opinions about the products and marks for flavour, colour, shape, packaging, and so on. This is called **sensory analysis**.

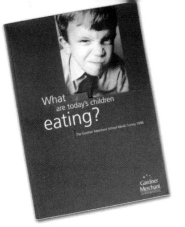

Surveys provide market researchers with useful information.

▶ Using the results of surveys published by other people and organizations, for example The National Food Survey, MORI, Sodexho.

Stage 2: What should the new product be like?

The manufacturer has to write down a list called a **specification**. The **first (initial)** specification may be changed as the product goes through the design process. The **final** specification is the one that will be used to make the product that will be sold. The manufacturer includes:

All the things they *want* included in the new product, for example:	**The manufacturer also has to specify all the things the law says they *must*, or *cannot*, include in the new product, for example:**
▶ its shape and size ▶ its flavour and colour ▶ what it will be used for, for example, a snack, a main meal, a party food ▶ what ingredients it will contain ▶ what nutrients it will contain ▶ how it will be made ▶ how it will be packaged and stored ▶ who it will be advertised to, for example children, teenagers, single people (this is called the **target group**) ▶ what it will cost to make and the price it will sell at ▶ what 'image' it will have, for example everyday, luxury, fashionable, reliable, versatile (lots of uses)	***cannot*** ▶ a certain amount or type of nutrient, for example sugar or fat ▶ a certain type of additive, for example a colour or preservative ▶ a particular method of preserving or packaging it ▶ a particular way of advertising it ***must*** ▶ certain information on the label

A specification may include a sketch.

CARTON
80 mm
70 mm
20 mm
LABEL
CHERRY Flavour
Bio Yogurt
55 mm
Best before: see lid
200 mm

Size: 75 g

Shape: round pot, 80 mm diameter.

Flavour: natural fruit flavouring from added fruit. Minimum added sugar.

Colour: natural colouring from added fruit

Use: part of main meal for older babies, toddlers and pre-school children

Ingredients: pasteurised, whole milk, pureed fresh fruit, sugar

Nutrients: those found in whole milk plus vitamins, minerals, and fibre from fruit; carbohydrate from sugar

Manufacture: added fruit to be stirred into set yogurt before packaging

Packaging: Plastic pot with easy to remove plastic lids, in packs of 6 with cardboard sleeve. Colourful cartoon characters on label.

Storage: chiller cabinet, can be frozen

Target group: parents and child carers of older babies, toddlers and pre-school children

Cost: manufacture: approximately 22p, recommended retail price: 29p

Image: healthy, easy to use, an aid to a baby learning to feed itself, right size for small appetites

Advertising: baby magazines, 'women's' magazines, afternoon and early evening TV

Samples of new food products are carefully tested before a final specification is drawn up.

A scientist tests a food sample for the presence of micro-organisms, which can make food unsafe to eat.

Stage 3: Developing the new product

Samples of the new product will be made and tested to see:
▶ how it tastes, smells and feels
▶ what it looks like
▶ what happens when it is cooked
▶ how well it can be stored
▶ how best to package it

Some of the ingredients, or the amounts used, may need to be changed to improve the product, for example, its flavour, texture or image. A **final specification** will be produced once the results of the tests are known.

Stage 4: Making the product

The real product, complete with all its packaging, will now be made. This is often called the **prototype**. As the prototype is being made, information is collected to see whether there are any problems with how it is made, or the machinery, ingredients, or packaging used.

One very important piece of information is how **safe** the food product is to eat. Food can be made unsafe to eat by tiny forms of life called **micro-organisms** (often called germs). These can get into the food if it is not carefully made and will cause **food poisoning**. The food manufacturer must check all stages of production to make sure that micro-organisms are not allowed to grow in the product while it is being made, or afterwards, while it is being stored.

Stage 5: Judging the product

The product is tested and judged by trained people and ordinary members of the public. This process is sometimes called 'evaluating'. The manufacturer will use their judgments and the results of the tests to make a final decision about making and selling the new product in the shops.

Stage 6: Putting the product on sale

The food manufacturer might decide to advertise and sell the new food product in one particular area of the country, to see how well it sells. This is called a **product trial**. If it sells well, it will be sold elsewhere.

If the product doesn't sell well, it may be tried in a different area or taken out of production. Or it may need to have flavour or colour improved. Sometimes, food products that have been on sale for a long time are changed slightly and sold as a 'new, improved' product to encourage people to buy more of them.

An important point for the manufacturer to consider is how to move products from one place to another (**distribution**). This includes:

▶ collecting raw materials (ingredients and packaging materials) or having them regularly delivered by suppliers

▶ storing finished food products

▶ sending out the finished products to shops, restaurants, warehouses and so on in good condition and on time.

A shopper samples a new food product in a supermarket. Manufacturers use the opinions of consumers to evaluate new products.

QUESTIONS

1 Why might a food manufacturer decide to design and produce a new food product?

2 Why is market research important to a food manufacturer?

3 Make up a specification for one of the following types of food product:
   a) a savoury fried potato snack
   b) a vegetarian soup
   c) a cold dessert based on bananas
   d) a healthy drink based on milk

4 Give the product (from question **3**) a name, and write down how you would test it to see whether people like it.

5 Make a list of some new food products that are available.

6 Make a list of some food products that have been improved, and state what has been done to improve them.

7 List the ways in which a manufacturer might encourage you to try a new product.

8 Which groups of people might need or want to buy these new products:
   a) frozen complete meals for one
   b) meat-free main meals
   c) easy-to-open snack-size cheese portions?

INTRODUCTION

PROJECT Novelty cake-making

Novelty cakes such as birthday cakes can be bought ready-made from a supermarket or ordered from a specialist cake shop.

Decorated cakes are used to celebrate a variety of occasions all over the world. The baking of a wedding cake, for example, is thought to be an ancient custom, as there is evidence that the ancient Greeks, and later the Romans, made cakes to celebrate weddings over 3,000 years ago!

Today, many celebration cakes are made in **specialist cake shops** by trained and experienced decorators. Customers plan the design of the cake they want with advice and ideas provided by staff at the shop. The cake is then made specially for that customer as a 'one-off' product.

Many of the processes used to make the cake are carried out by hand, require great skill and are time-consuming, for example, making sugar flowers and models, painting and piping the icing. This has to be included in the charge made for each cake.

Cake decorators use a range of equipment to create different designs:

Cake decorating tools

Tool	Use
Plastic rolling pin	for rolling out ready-made icing (sugar paste) or marzipan
Craft knife	for cutting out accurate shapes in icing
Ball tool	for modelling and frilling the edges of pieces of icing
Plastic and metal cutters	in a variety of shapes to make cake decorations, flowers, models, etc.
Crimpers	used like tweezers to create a decorative pattern on the edge or surface of rolled-out icing
Paint brushes	to create decorative patterns, pictures or writing using food colourings
Piping bags and nozzles	to create a variety of decorations and designs using royal icing
Plastic moulds	to create easy-to-make and accurate decorations e.g. animals, faces, flowers, fruits
Concentrated paste colours	to colour icing, marzipan, and for painting
Icing sugar shaker	to spread an even amount of sugar on the work surface
Palette knife	for lifting icing shapes easily from the work surface
Icing smoothers	for making a smooth, flat surface on a cake using sugar paste
Ready-made decorations and components	to make quick and effective designs on cakes

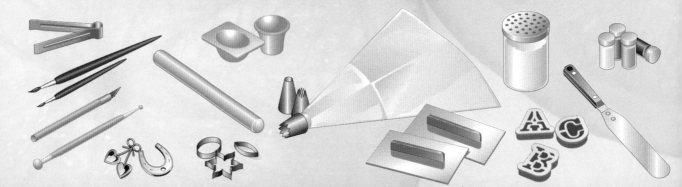

It is also possible to buy **ready-made** celebration cakes from supermarkets. These are produced in factories in large numbers, using a range of designs to suit a variety of age groups, themes and occasions. Some of the processes used to make these cakes are performed by machine, and some by hand. As they are made in large numbers, these cakes are usually lower in price than those made in specialist shops.

A simple sponge cake can be shaped and decorated in many different ways to make an attractive novelty cake.

Brief

Using a ready-made sponge or fruit cake and ready-made roll-out icing (sugar paste), design and decorate a novelty celebration cake for a special occasion. Remember that fruit cakes must be covered with marzipan (almond paste) before they are iced, to stop the fruit cake staining the icing brown. Before adding the roll-out icing, brush the marzipan with a little water, so that the icing will stick to it. Sponge cakes can be covered with butter icing or jam before the roll-out icing is put on.

Ready-made roll-out icing should be kneaded until it is soft and smooth, then rolled out on some icing sugar to stop it from sticking to the work surface. It should be turned often while being rolled out, then lifted carefully and draped over the cake. Finally, it should be smoothed onto the cake with the palms of the hands and fingers or an icing smoother.

Ready-made roll-out icing is easy to use and provides a smooth surface to which decorations can be added.

Research

❖ Identify the **theme** of your cake.
❖ Identify the **target group** for your cake.
❖ Sketch your ideas for designs.
❖ Investigate the equipment you could use and think about how it would make the production of your cake easier, less time-consuming and more 'professional' in appearance.
❖ Investigate the ready-made decorations and components you could use.
❖ Suggest how your design could be made on a large scale in a factory.
❖ Find out the possible health problems associated with using food colourings.

Your specification

Write down what the product will be like:
▸ What size and shape will it be?
▸ Will it be a fruit or a sponge cake?
▸ Make a sketch of the final design.
▸ How would it be packaged for sale in a shop?
▸ How would it be stored in a shop?

Unit 1 Understanding ingredients

By the end of this section, you should be able to:
- Identify how to choose ingredients.
- Understand the importance of working accurately, safely, tidily and hygienically when handling food in the home and in industry.

Organizing your practical work

Choosing ingredients

To make a good food product you need to start with good quality ingredients.

Here is a checklist to help you choose:

Food	What to look for	What to avoid
Fresh fruit	▸ should be just ripe ▸ should be a good colour	▸ over-ripe, soft, mushy fruit ▸ bruises, cuts, moulds on the outside
Fresh vegetables	▸ should be a good colour, e.g. green leaves with no yellowing	▸ wilting, wrinkly leaves and skins ▸ green potatoes ▸ sprouting potatoes, onions, and so on
Cheese, milk, cream, yogurt	▸ the use-by date must not have passed ▸ how much fat they contain (look at the label) ▸ soya alternatives for people with cow's milk allergies	▸ mouldy cheese ▸ out-of-date products ▸ full-fat ingredients for a reduced-fat product
Fresh meat (raw)	▸ more lean meat than fat ▸ cheaper cuts for stews, casseroles ▸ not too much bone ▸ moist, not wet ▸ fresh smell, springy flesh ▸ the use-by date must not have passed	▸ colour changed to green/brown ▸ slimy, wet meat ▸ 'off' smell ▸ out-of-date products
Fresh fish (raw)	▸ bright eyes, shiny scales ▸ moist skin, firm flesh ▸ fresh smell ▸ bright red gills	▸ sunken, dull eyes ▸ slimy skin, loose scales ▸ strong, unpleasant fishy smell ▸ sunken gills
Canned, bottled and dried foods	▸ 'best before' date must not have passed ▸ cans and packets must be in good condition	▸ dented, rusty, or bulging cans ▸ split, damp packets ▸ out-of-date products ▸ containers with broken seals

People who work with food should wear protective overalls, a head covering and gloves.

Organizing yourself and your workplace

Are you ready to work with food? Use this checklist to find out:

You	Your workplace
hands washed	work surface clean and tidy
nails clean	all equipment to hand
clean apron	ingredients weighed
long hair tied back	cleaning equipment ready
sleeves rolled up	plan of work to hand

Good working practices

To be successful when you prepare and produce food products, there are some simple rules to follow. Use the checklist below to see how good your working practices are:

Accuracy
- Use scales to weigh ingredients.
- Measure liquids on a level surface.
- Use proper spoon measures.

Safety
- Use sharp knives, never blunt ones.
- When walking with a knife, hold it at your side, blade pointing down, by the handle.
- Chop food on a board, away from your body.
- Follow the instructions for using mixers, microwave ovens, and so on.
- Wear oven gloves to put in and take items out of the oven.
- Wipe up spills from the floor.
- Do not run in the workplace.
- Keep fabrics away from flames.
- Do not let pan handles stick out from the hob.
- Work tidily.

Hygiene
- Do not sneeze, spit or cough over food.
- Do not smoke near food.
- Wash your hands after using the toilet.
- Keep meat, fish, milk, cream, yogurt and cheese cool.
- Keep raw foods away from cooked foods.
- Wash fruit and vegetables thoroughly.
- Cover up cuts, grazes and skin infections.
- Do not lick your fingers or kitchen tools.
- Wash up with hot, soapy water and make sure everything is clean.
- Wipe down work surfaces, the cooker and the sink.
- Wash tea towels and dishcloths regularly.

Organizing practical work in the food industry

Anyone working in the food industry should follow the rules above, as well as those below:

Workers	Ingredients	Equipment and workplace
clean uniforms	carefully selected	regularly maintained
hats to cover hair	cleaned and correctly stored	safely used
clean, covered hands	accurately weighed/measured	thoroughly and regularly cleaned
well trained	regularly checked for quality	regularly checked for signs of wear
health regularly checked	regular checks on finished products	well organized so the food passes easily from one stage to the next

Unit ① Food science

By the end of this section, you should be able to:

▶ Understand what food science means.

▶ Identify some of the ways in which foods change their appearance, colour, texture, flavour and smell when prepared, chilled and cooked.

Some foods can be eaten raw, while others are cooked to make them easier and nicer to eat. Some foods are mixed with other foods to make a different food product.

Food science is the study of what happens to foods when they are cut, whisked, melted, frozen, cooked, left in the open air, or mixed with other foods. Some changes to foods can be seen with the naked eye, some cannot.

Understanding how foods change will help you to understand what has happened if your cooking goes wrong and to design new food products.

How foods change

Action	Example of food	What happens?	Why?
Cutting	apples	the apple goes brown	the air mixes (reacts) with **enzymes** (substances in the apple), which makes it go brown
	cabbage	some of the vitamin C is lost	the vitamin C in the cabbage reacts with the air and is destroyed
Whisking	egg whites, eggs and sugar	air is trapped in small bubbles	protein in the egg stretches and holds lots of air
	whipping or double cream	the cream changes from a liquid to a thick texture and holds its shape	tiny drops of fat in the cream gradually stick together
Melting	chocolate margarine	the fat in each changes from solid to liquid	the heat changes the structure of the fat; when it cools down, the fat will go solid again
Freezing	meat	the meat becomes solid	tiny ice crystals form in the meat cells; some of the cell walls break and liquid leaks from them when the meat thaws
	ice-cream	the texture becomes smooth and foamy	as the mixture is stirred, tiny ice crystals form around lots of tiny air bubbles
	strawberries	the strawberries become mushy and soft when they thaw	ice crystals break down the cell walls so they can't hold their shape when they thaw
Cooking	fried eggs	the clear white becomes opaque and sets and the yolk becomes solid	the protein in the egg gradually sets as it is heated; the yolk takes longer than the white

Action	Example of food	What happens?	Why?
Cooking	cake mixture	cake changes from a soft, semi-liquid into a solid sponge with a light brown crust	‣ the fat melts and is absorbed by the starch in the flour ‣ air bubbles in the mixture expand and make the cake rise ‣ the sugar melts and helps make the cake golden brown in colour ‣ the eggs set ‣ the protein in the flour sets
	boiled rice, pasta, potatoes, yams, cassava	the texture changes from hard to soft	‣ starch granules absorb water, swell up and soften
	red meat	the texture becomes tender the colour changes to brown the flavour develops	‣ collagen (a protein) changes to gelatine and softens the meat ‣ heat causes a chemical reaction that changes the colour ‣ substances called **extractives** are squeezed out of the meat onto its surface and give it flavour
	jam	the fruit is stewed in water, then boiled with sugar until it forms a 'gel', which sets when the jam cools down	‣ a substance in the fruit called **pectin** traps the water, sugar and fruit in a 3-D network (the gel); there has to be enough pectin in the fruit to make this happen
	bread	‣ yeast is mixed with warm water and sugar ‣ strong plain flour, yeast and water are mixed to an elastic dough and kneaded ‣ the dough is left to rise in a warm place ‣ the bread is baked in a hot oven and changes from a soft dough to a solid crusty loaf	‣ bubbles of carbon dioxide (CO_2) gas appear as the yeast breaks down the sugar ‣ gluten (a protein) in the flour forms long chains when water is added and makes the dough stretchy ‣ yeast breaks down natural sugars in the flour to make CO_2 gas, which pushes the elastic dough up ‣ the bread rises quickly as the CO_2 gas expands and pushes up the dough ‣ the yeast is eventually killed ‣ the water is absorbed by starch in the flour ‣ the gluten sets to form the structure of the bread ‣ water, CO_2 gas and alcohol (made by the yeast) escape from the bread

Action	Example of food	What happens?	Why?
Mixing	Lemon juice, cream and condensed milk	the mixture becomes thick and if poured onto a biscuit base and chilled can be cut into slices	the acid in the lemon juice reacts with the protein in the milk and cream and makes it set
	Egg yolk, oil and vinegar to make mayonnaise	the mixture gradually thickens as the oil is slowly added and the oil does not separate out	a substance in the egg yolk called **lecithin** prevents the oil and vinegar separating by emulsifying them. The lecithin is an emulsifier. Emulsifiers are used a great deal in processed foods

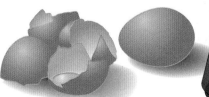

QUESTIONS

1 Make a list of foods that:
  ▶ are usually eaten raw
  ▶ are usually eaten cooked
  ▶ can be eaten raw or cooked
2 Find out how you can prevent the following from happening:
  ▶ cut apples turning brown
  ▶ vitamin C being lost from cut cabbage
  ▶ a cake sinking when removed from the oven
  ▶ whipped cream separating into butter and liquid
3 Find out what has gone wrong with the following and how the problem could have been prevented:
  ▶ bread that is very heavy and has hardly risen
  ▶ mayonnaise that has separated
  ▶ jam that has not set
  ▶ cooked rice that is very sticky
  ▶ a cheese sauce that is very lumpy
  ▶ flaky pastry that has not risen and is very greasy

Unit  1

Foods to suit different needs

By the end of this section, you should be able to:

▶ Understand how putting different foods together can help you to follow current dietary advice for healthy eating.
▶ Identify combinations of foods that are suitable for different needs.

Lots of research has been carried out to find out the best way to enjoy a healthy life. The current advice for people (from young children to adults) who want to stay healthy is:

▶ Eat less sugar and sugary foods
▶ Eat less fat – especially solid fats from animals
▶ Eat less salt and salty foods
▶ Drink less alcohol
▶ Eat more dietary fibre and starchy foods
▶ Eat lots of fruit and vegetables – at least 5 portions a day – fresh, frozen or canned (and not just potatoes)
▶ Eat a mixture of foods
▶ Enjoy your food
▶ Try to stay at a healthy weight
▶ Be more active, e.g.
   walk, rather than ride in a car
   use the stairs, not the lift or escalator
   take up a sport such as swimming or football
   don't spend too much time sitting in front of the TV or playing computer games

Fresh fruit is a source of vitamins, carbohydrates and minerals and is an essential part of a healthy diet.

It can be difficult to work out how much fat, sugar or other nutrient is in a food product just by looking at the nutrition information on the label. Some food manufacturers and retailers try to help consumers to choose healthy foods by putting logos or symbols on food products, indicating that they are, for example, 'full fat' or low in sugar. Sometimes a product that says it is low in fat may actually be high in something else, for example sugar, so it is important to find out more about foods so that you can make good choices.

Reduced-fat and reduced-sugar foods are among the many products available to health-conscious consumers.

The list of foods in the table below is a guide that will help you to identify combinations of foods that could be used to provide a balanced diet, or a diet for someone with special needs:

A healthy diet

Meal	High energy	High fibre	High iron	High vitamin C	High calcium
Breakfasts	breads pancakes cereals porridge nuts, dried fruit buns, croissants fried foods full-cream milk	wholegrain cereals wholemeal breads fresh fruit dried fruit beans, pulses	wholegrain cereals fortified cereals (iron added) red meats liver, kidneys dried apricots wholegrain breads	fresh fruit e.g. oranges, grapefruit, kiwi fruit fruit and vegetable juices	milk yogurt cheeses fortified cereals and milks beans, pulses
	Low fat	Low salt	Low sugar	Vegetarian	
Breakfasts	yogurts made with low-fat milk fresh fruits plain breads crisp breads 100% wholegrain breakfast cereals skimmed or semi-skimmed milk low-fat spreads white fish lean meats	'No added salt' breakfast cereals fresh fruit natural yogurts low-salt baked beans, margarine, butter	'No added sugar' breakfast cereals reduced or sugar-free jams and spreads fresh fruit plain breads natural yogurts reduced-sugar fruit yogurts natural (not concentrated) fruit juices	eggs – fried, poached, scrambled, boiled, omelette cheeses beans, pulses, lentils breads, cereals fresh and dried fruits nuts	

A nutritious cooked breakfast for a vegetarian

A breakfast that is rich in both calcium and fibre

LOW FAT

CHERRY flavour yogurt

A healthy diet

	High energy	High fibre	High iron	High vitamin C	High calcium
Lunches/ Dinners	breads (sandwiches, pittas, pizzas) meats fried foods pastries pasta, rice fats, cheese, cream	fruits vegetables wholegrain rice, pasta beans, lentils dried fruits wholemeal bread, flour	curry spices red meats liver, kidney, heart wholemeal flour, cereals poppadams dried apricots chocolate	citrus fruits peppers kiwi fruit blackcurrants beansprouts broccoli cabbage spinach	milk cheese yogurt bread bones of canned fish green vegetables wholegrain cereals beans, pulses

	Low fat	Low salt	Low sugar	Vegetarian	
Lunches/ Dinners	lean meats white fish skimmed milk fresh fruit (except avocados) fresh vegetables wholemeal breads and cereals poultry	natural low-fat yogurt fruit and vegetables	fresh fruit vegetables plain breads reduced sugar or 'diet' yogurts and drinks	vegetable soups, stews, curries, pies, pasties pasta with sauces rice and beans nuts breads wheat and soya flour products meat substitutes e.g. Quorn and tofu	

A convenient, high-energy lunch or dinner

A light, low-fat meal

QUESTIONS

1 Using the lists above, write out a menu for a day's meals for each of the following people:
   a) a teenage girl who needs extra iron
   b) a teenage boy who is growing fast and takes part in lots of sports
   c) a pregnant vegetarian woman who needs extra iron, calcium and B vitamins
   d) an elderly man who is not very active but enjoys cooking
   e) an overweight man with heart disease, who has been told to eat less fat and salt
   f) a teenage diabetic girl who has to reduce the amount of sugar and increase the amount of fibre and starchy foods she eats

2 Design some logos for a large food retailer who wants to promote 'own brand' products that meet the guidelines for healthy eating, i.e. low in fat, low in sugar, high in fibre, low in salt.

Unit 1

Food production and the environment

By the end of this section, you should be able to:
- Identify the different effects food production has on the environment.
- Identify ways in which food producers, manufacturers and consumers can minimize these effects on the environment.

The environment

In Britain in the 20th century, the problems of food shortage during the Second World War and concerns about growing populations made the government encourage farmers to grow more and more food. To do this, farmers have used lots of inputs, such as:

- **chemicals** to kill insects, animals, weeds and diseases (these chemicals are called pesticides)
- **chemical fertilizers** to put nutrients back into the soil
- **man-made, enriched animal feeds** to make animals grow quickly and cheaply
- **antibiotics and other medicines** to prevent disease and make animals grow quickly
- **tractors and farm machinery** to do jobs quickly and with fewer people and working animals

Farmers spray their crops to keep them free of weeds and protect them from pests and diseases.

Many inputs and modern farming methods have had very serious and long-term effects on the environment, including:

- hedgerows, ponds, woodlands, rainforests and other natural habitats have been destroyed to make way for big fields and plantations for crops, and grazing land for animals
- soils have had water, nutrients, and goodness taken out of them, and not replaced
- water ways (rivers, streams, lakes, ponds and seas) have been polluted with pesticides, fertilizers and animal waste
- many types of insects, birds, fish and other animals have died out because they either have been poisoned by chemicals or have lost their natural food sources or habitats
- important materials, like oil and minerals, have been taken from the Earth. They are **non-renewable** (cannot be replaced)

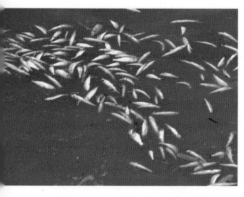

Chemicals used in farming can get washed into rivers by rain, poisoning the water and killing wildlife.

People have also been affected, because:

- there are not so many jobs available in farming as there are fewer (but larger) farms, and much of the work is done by machines, not people
- many rural (countryside) communities have disappeared as farms have gone
- they have become ill, because of farm chemicals in their food or drinking water
- **intensive farming** (where lots of animals are kept together inside in small places) has led to diseases passing from one animal to another, and sometimes to humans

Food manufacturers have also had a big impact on the environment, because:

▶ they use lots of non-renewable energy sources to produce, store and distribute (for example by lorry or aeroplane) their products

▶ they use lots of packaging materials, for example paper, plastics, card, metal and glass, which use energy to make and end up as rubbish, which has to be disposed of

Intensive farming means that meat and other products can be produced more cheaply, but can lead to the spread of disease.

One of the causes of environmental pollution is the transport of food from the farm to the consumer's home, which may involve ships, aeroplanes, lorries and cars. Some people have called this 'food miles', and some foods travel very long distances.

One of the reasons for this is that large supermarket companies use big **distribution warehouses**, to which food products are sent. They are then sent out from there to individual supermarkets. Another reason is that consumers have become used to having different foods available all year round, so many have to be imported by air or sea from all over the world.

Food travels

▶ In the USA, it is estimated that, on average, each food item travels 2,000 kilometres.

▶ In the UK, bananas imported into Southampton are taken to Lancashire (by road) for ripening, then to a warehouse in Somerset, and then to supermarkets all over Britain (including Southampton).

▶ In southern Germany, a yogurt distributor imports strawberries from Poland, yogurt from northern Germany, maize and wheat flour from The Netherlands, jam from West Germany, and sugar from East Germany. This means that a pot of yogurt travels 1,005 kilometres before it is eaten.

Preventing damage to the environment

There are many ways in which food producers, manufacturers, retailers and consumers can help to prevent damage to the environment:

Producers

It is possible for farmers to produce food without using chemical inputs or medicines. They can do this by:

▶ keeping the soil in good condition by using natural fertilizers such as manure

▶ growing a different crop on the same piece of land each year, and then letting the land rest for a year (called **crop rotation**)

▶ using other insects to control insects that damage crops (for example, ladybirds eat greenfly (aphids)

Free-range chickens are raised outdoors, unlike intensively farmed chickens, which are kept indoors.

▶ removing weeds by hand or by machine
▶ growing crops that suit local conditions, such as soil, weather and rainfall
▶ allowing animals to live as naturally as possible

This type of farming is called **organic farming**. The food produced is, as far as possible, free from added chemicals. Recent food scares and concern about health and the environment have encouraged a growing number of farmers to convert to organic farming. Organic food usually costs more to produce and buy, but as demand grows, prices should gradually come down.

Manufacturers and retailers
They can help the environment by:
▶ using local suppliers of food, so cutting down food miles
▶ using less packaging
▶ using recycled materials for packaging
▶ supporting organic farmers
▶ listening to consumer demands and concerns about the environment
▶ locating more shops in towns so people don't have to travel so far to shop for food

Consumers
They can help the environment by:
▶ buying food that is locally grown
▶ buying food with minimum packaging
▶ supporting organic farmers where possible
▶ recycling packaging
▶ using biodegradable washing-up liquid and washing powders to help prevent water pollution

Organic farmers avoid the use of chemicals and produce their crops using only natural fertilizers and pest control methods.

Most supermarkets sell organic produce including fruit, vegetables and meat. Although such produce is more expensive to buy, many people believe that it tastes better and is safer to eat.

QUESTIONS

1 Carry out a survey of fruit and vegetables at your local supermarket and find out:
   a) which ones are imported from other countries
   b) which ones could be grown in the UK but have been imported
   c) which fruit or vegetable has travelled the most food miles
2 Carry out a survey of packaging for one of the following food product categories:
   a) biscuits and cookies
   b) cakes
   c) ready-made main meals
   d) savoury snacks
   ▶ Which product has the most and which the least packaging?
   ▶ For each product, why has that particular packaging been used?
   ▶ Which packaging do you consider to be unnecessary?
   ▶ How easy or difficult is it to open the packaging?
   ▶ How environmentally friendly is the packaging?
     (Is it made from recycled materials? Can it be recycled?
     How long will it take to disappear in a rubbish tip?)
3 Carry out a survey to find out how many types of organic food are sold in your local supermarket. How well are they marked to show that they are organic and how do their prices compare with similar non-organic foods?
4 Find out how supermarket companies and organizations such as the RSPCA are trying to improve the lives of farm animals.

PROJECT Salads

Many restaurants have a salad bar from which customers can help themselves.

Salads are a popular and healthy food product and are used in a variety of ways, for example:

◗ as a starter to a meal
◗ as a complete main meal
◗ as an accompaniment to a meal
◗ as a filling for sandwiches or rolls

Salads can include raw vegetables, herbs and fruits; cooked foods such as rice, pasta, eggs, meat, fish and potatoes; nuts, pulses, beans and dried fruits and pickles and dressings. Some of the most common salad ingredients, and how to prepare them, are listed in the chart opposite.

Brief

A supermarket chain plans to introduce a new range of salads with 'colour' as the theme. Design a set of salads, each based on a different colour, for example red, orange, green or yellow, that could be sold in two-, four- or six-portion sizes. Design the packaging and advertising poster to go with the salad range. Prepare two of your designs.

Research

❖ Why are salads healthy?
❖ Why are salads an easy food product to use?
❖ When can salads be eaten?
❖ What can be served with salads?
❖ How should salad ingredients be prepared and stored to make them safe to eat? What are the reasons for this?
❖ What types of packaging are suitable for salads?
❖ What unusual fruits and vegetables could be used in salads?
❖ What information should the packaging give the consumer?

Your specification

Write down what your products will be like:

◗ Will they be vegetarian or non-vegetarian?
◗ Will they be packaged in a carton or a bag?
◗ What portion size will they be?
◗ What ingredients will they include?
◗ How will they meet the requirements of the brief?
◗ What information will the packaging give and how will it attract consumers?

Your ideas

Use recipe books, leaflets and cards to find ideas. You can also look in magazines, supermarkets and salad bars for ideas. Write down your ideas and those of your friends (brainstorming). Invent names for your products. Choose two or three products to make.

Develop your ideas

Make the products you have chosen. Set up a tasting panel and ask your friends to give your salads scores on flavour, texture, colour and appeal. Choose one idea. Use the results from the tasting panel to change or improve the product if necessary.

Make a final product specification

Find out how a similar product would be made in industry, and how it would be packaged, labelled and sold in the shops.

Making and evaluating

Make the product and evaluate it to see whether it answers the brief and fits the specification.

Preparing salad ingredients

Raw vegetables

Lettuce   Discard outer, damaged leaves. Wash well and dry. Tear leaves or leave them whole.

Watercress   Discard damaged leaves and thick stalks. Wash well and dry.

Cucumber   Wash the skin or remove it with a vegetable peeler. Slice thinly.

Spring onion   Remove roots and outer skin. Wash well. Cut tops off.

Tomato   Wash well. Cut into slices or segments.

Celery   Trim off leaves and root ends. Scrub each stalk well and slice or cut into sticks.

Pepper (capsicum)   Wash well. Cut in half lengthways and remove core, seeds and pith. Cut into slices or dice (small pieces).

Carrot   Wash well. Serve whole, if small, or grate or slice.

Mushrooms   Wash, peel if necessary, and slice thinly.

Cabbage   Shred finely and wash well.

Bean sprouts   Wash well. Serve whole or chopped.

Cooked vegetables

Potato   Cut into dice to make potato salad, or serve new potatoes hot with mint and butter.

Carrots   Cut into dice and add to potato salad.

Beans

Red kidney beans, haricot beans, butter beans   Soak dried beans overnight in cold water, then boil for at least 20 minutes, until soft.

Broad beans   Wash and boil gently for 15 minutes, until soft.

French beans, runner beans Boil until soft and serve with a dressing.

Fresh fruits

Apple   Leave skin on. Slice and core, sprinkle with lemon juice to prevent browning.

Banana   Peel, slice and sprinkle with lemon juice.

Citrus fruits   Peel, remove segments and discard pips and pith.

Pineapple   Peel and remove hard core, slice or cube.

Dried fruits

Apricots, raisins, mangoes, apples, etc. Use whole or chopped.

Nuts

Almonds   Use blanched, flaked or toasted almonds.

Walnuts, peanuts, cashew nuts, hazel nuts, Brazil nuts   Use whole or chopped.

PROJECT Soups

The word 'soup' comes from an old French word meaning 'a piece of bread soaked in liquid'. In the past, soups were served in many homes as a whole meal and would have had vegetables and cereals (like barley and oats) in them, and sometimes meat or fish. They would have been served with bread to provide a warm, filling meal.

Nowadays, soups are usually served as an addition to a meal, for example as a starter, or as part of a midday meal with sandwiches. They can be home-made or ready-made.

Ready-made soups are available in a number of forms:

dried   just add boiling water, or add water and simmer for a few minutes (also available from vending machines)

canned heat in a pan or microwave

fresh   to be heated in a pan or microwave; fresh soups have a short shelf-life.

Different cultures have traditional soup recipes, many of which are available ready-made, for example:

minestrone from Italy
Scotch broth from Scotland
bortsch from Eastern Europe
vichyssoise from France
chicken and sweetcorn soup from China

Dried soups are available from vending machines.

Canned soups have a long shelf-life.

Fresh soups should be kept refrigerated.

Soups can be grouped according to how they are prepared, cooked and served:

Smooth soups The ingredients are cooked with a liquid and then everything is liquidized together, until smooth (before liquidizers were invented, the mixture had to be rubbed through a sieve to make it smooth).

'Chunky' soups The ingredients are cut into small pieces (so several at a time can fit onto a spoon) and cooked in the liquid until tender.

Chilled soups The ingredients are either cooked very lightly or not at all, then chilled. These soups are often smooth but do not have to be.

Clear soups The cooking liquid is transparent, so you can see all the other ingredients floating in the soup.

Briefs

Choose one of the following:

1. A local charity wishes to set up a soup kitchen to provide warm food for homeless people. They hope to serve two types of soup, which will be made by volunteers in a mobile kitchen. Choose two soups that would be suitable for this project.
2. A sandwich bar in a city centre wants to extend its range of foods by offering take-away soups. It already caters for a variety of ethnic groups and also offers vegetarian choices. Design a soup menu for the sandwich bar that will cater for the needs of its customers.
3. A local authority has cut out hot midday meals in its secondary schools, and now only offers filled rolls, cakes and fruit. One school wishes to offer hot, take-away soups in the winter, but only has facilities to offer two varieties each day. Prepare two soups that would meet the needs and preferences of most of the pupils and staff in the school. Design a poster to attract pupils to this addition to their midday meal choices.

Research

❖ What are the particular needs of the target group in the brief you have chosen?
❖ If appropriate, conduct a survey to find out what kinds of soup people prefer.

Your specification

Write down what your products will be like:

▶ Will they be vegetarian or non-vegetarian?
▶ How much would you serve in one portion?
▶ What would the soups cost to make per portion, and how much would they be sold for?
▶ What could be served with the soups?
▶ How would the soups be prepared, served and packaged?
▶ How would the soups be kept appetizing and safe to eat during preparation, cooking and serving?

A thick, chunky vegetable soup, served with bread, makes a filling meal.

Unit ② Designing and making for yourself

Designing food products

Recipes

A **recipe** is a list of ingredients and instructions for making the ingredients into a food product. All over the world, thousands of recipes have been invented over the years, and many of these have become part of the traditional food culture of different countries. In modern food technology, a recipe is often called the 'product specification', and ingredients may be called 'components'. Food manufacturers design and use specifications for each product they make.

All food products are made from one of a number of basic recipes. They can be divided into the following groups:

▸ **Sauces** Made with flour, cornflour, egg, cream, fruits, tomatoes, meat or fish juices
▸ **Cakes and biscuits** Made by beating, mixing, whisking, or melting the ingredients
▸ **Pastries** Made by melting, mixing, kneading or folding the ingredients
▸ **Stews, casseroles, soups, curries** Made with meats, fish, vegetables, beans, pulses, grains, fruits, spices and herbs
▸ **Fried foods** Meats, poultry, fish, vegetables, cereal products, fruits
▸ **Breads** Made with different cereal grains, with or without yeast
▸ **Cereal products** Pastas, noodles, breakfast cereals, snacks
▸ **Pies, patties, flans, tarts, parcels** Containing meats, vegetables, fruits, preserves, fish
▸ **Confectionery** Jellies, chocolates, syrups, candies, gums, toffees, roots (e.g. liquorice), candied fruits and nuts, etc.
▸ **Desserts, puddings** Made with cereals, fruits, dairy products, chocolate, fats, honey, etc.
▸ **Drinks (beverages)** Made with infusions of leaves or roasted beans, dairy products, fruits, herbs, spices, alcohol, etc.

Adapting food products

It may sometimes be necessary to adapt (change) the recipe of a food product for a number of reasons:

- to make it more suitable for people wanting to follow healthy eating guidelines, for example by reducing the sugar content
- to produce another product in the same range, but with a different flavour or texture
- to give a product a new image
- to find a new target group for the product
- to reduce the cost of the product
- to find an alternative for an ingredient that is becoming difficult to obtain

Many manufacturers have adapted their products to cater for consumers with special needs, for example vegetarians or those who want to reduce their fat or sugar intake.

Most recipes can be adapted by:
- replacing one or more of the ingredients with another
- reducing or increasing the amount of one or more of the ingredients
- using a different additive, for example, a colouring or a flavouring

Changing a recipe in some way may cause problems, for example:
- it may affect the shelf-life of the product (how long it stays fit and safe to eat)
- it may affect how acceptable it is to consumers (they might not like the change and stop buying the product)

QUESTIONS

1 Make a list of four countries and write down as many recipes as you can think of that are traditional in each.
2 What types of product have been adapted by food manufacturers to meet current healthy eating guidelines, which suggest that people should eat less fat, less sugar, less salt and more fibre? Give examples.
3 How would you adapt the following recipes?
   a) converting a meat curry or lasagne to a vegetarian one
   b) making a vegetable soup with less salt
   c) making a fruit cake with less added sugar

Unit 2

Processing and cooking food

By the end of this section, you should be able to:
- Understand why foods are processed and cooked.
- Identify ways in which foods are processed and cooked.
- Understand how new processing techniques have enabled the food industry to develop new products.

What is processing?

'Processing' means making a series of changes to something. **Food processing** changes some of the features of foods, including:

- how long they stay in a good and safe condition
- their colour, texture, flavour, appearance
- how long they take to prepare and cook
- how easy and convenient they are to use

Food processing has enabled the food industry to develop new products by:

- Making it possible to make several new products out of one food. For example, potatoes can be turned into chips, crisps, instant mashed potato, potato salad, canned potatoes, oven-baked shaped potato pieces, potato waffles.
- Making it possible to make products that are of the same standard and quality every time, so that consumers know what to expect and will buy them again.
- Making it possible to make foods **aesthetically pleasing** (nice to look at and appetizing).

How are foods processed?

There are a number of processes that are carried out in the kitchen as well as in industry. These include:

- trimming (e.g. vegetables, fish, meat)
- peeling, coring, slicing, chopping, mincing, grating (e.g. fruit, vegetables, meat, poultry, cheese, nuts)
- sieving, separating, crushing, rolling (e.g. flour, sugar, biscuits, spices, pastry, icing)
- whisking, mixing, beating, combining (e.g. cake, biscuit, bread and egg mixtures, soups)
- grilling, frying, baking, roasting, boiling, steaming, microwaving, poaching, stewing, simmering
- preserving by freezing, pickling or adding sugar or salt

In industry, processes that require specialist equipment and knowledge are also carried out. The chart opposite lists some of these, and shows why they are done. (The key to the left explains the symbols used.)

Heat-treating milk destroys micro-organisms.

Processing treatment	Reason	Examples
Cook–chill	Prevents growth of micro-organisms Convenience Makes food aesthetically pleasing	Ready-made meals
Modified atmosphere packaging	Prevents growth of micro-organisms Convenience Makes food aesthetically pleasing	Cooked meats, cheeses
Vacuum packaging	As above	
Irradiation	Destroys micro-organisms present in food Makes food aesthetically pleasing	

Key to symbols

- ⊛ prevents growth of micro-organisms
- ⋈ destroys micro-organisms present in food
- ⚲ changes the food into a different product
- removes impurities from food
- ⊙ convenience
- ⦶ prevents food from separating
- ⊕ breaks food down, so parts of it can be extracted (taken out)
- ✾ makes food aesthetically pleasing (attractive, appetizing)

Processing treatment	Symbols
Ultra heat treatment	⊛ ⋈ ⊙
Sterilization	⊛ ⋈
Pasteurization	⊛ ⋈ (some)
Condensing	⚲ ✾
Evaporating	⚲
Canning	⊛ ⋈ ⊙
Pickling	⊛ ⋈
Smoking/curing	⊛ ⋈
Adding salt	⊛ ⋈
Adding sugar	⊛ ⋈ ✾
Freezing	⊛ ⊙
Irradiation	⊛ ⋈ ✾
Dehydrating	⊛ ⋈
Freeze drying	⊛ ⋈
Colouring	✾
Adding flavouring	✾
Emulsifying	⦶
Stabilizing	⦶ ✾
Milling	⊙ ⊕
Refining	⚲ ✾
Pre-cooking	⊙ ✾
Pre-peeling/slicing/chopping	⊙ ✾
Adding raising agent	⚲ ⊙
Hydrogenating (adding hydrogen to vegetable oil to make solid fat)	⚲

The processes here are those most commonly used.

QUESTIONS

1. Complete the chart above by finding out some examples of foods that are processed in each way (a few have been done for you).
2. Find out why the processes of pickling, adding sugar and adding salt are used.
3. Make a list of food products that are made using the following foods: wheat, rice, milk, soya beans
4. Why are the following processes carried out only in the food industry and not at home?
   ▸ pasteurization ▸ canning ▸ hydrogenating

Unit 2

Keeping food products safe to eat

By the end of this section, you should be able to:

▶ Understand what micro-organisms are and how they affect the safety of food.

▶ Identify ways of keeping food products safe to eat during their making, distribution, storage and use.

Every year, thousands of people suffer from **food poisoning**. Food poisoning is caused by **toxins** (poisons), which are produced in the food by tiny forms of life called **micro-organisms**. There are three main types of micro-organism:

▶ bacteria (these cause most of the cases of food poisoning)
▶ moulds
▶ yeasts

Not all bacteria, moulds and yeasts are harmful. Some are used in foods. For example, bacteria are used to make yogurt, moulds are used to make some cheeses, and yeast is used to make bread. Harmful micro-organisms are called **pathogenic** micro-organisms or **pathogens**.

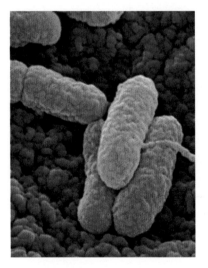

Salmonella bacteria

Bread mould

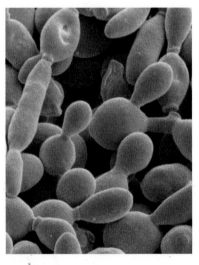

Yeast cells

How do micro-organisms get into foods?

Micro-organisms are very small (1 million bacteria can fit on a pin-head) and they are found in many different places, for example water, air, soil, dust, skin, the nose, throat and mouth, sewage, rubbish, animals, foods. This means that they can easily **contaminate** (be passed on to) food, in the following ways:

▶ by sneezing, spitting or coughing near food
▶ by not washing the hands after using the toilet or touching the inside of the nose or a used handkerchief or tissue
▶ by not washing dirty vegetables properly

- by not washing dirty animals before slaughtering them for meat
- by allowing animals near food while it is being prepared
- by allowing a kitchen to become dirty
- by keeping rubbish near food
- by storing raw and cooked meats, poultry or fish next to each other
- by feeding animals with contaminated feed-stuffs
- by leaving food exposed to the air, dust and flies
- by wearing dirty clothing when handling food

How do micro-organisms cause food poisoning?

If micro-organisms are given the right conditions — i.e. temperature (usually warm), moisture and food — they will grow and multiply quickly. As they do so, they produce toxins (poisons), which can make people very sick if they eat the food. Very perishable foods (see p112) are the most likely to be contaminated by micro-organisms and associated with food poisoning.

Although it is often impossible to see whether food has been contaminated with bacteria, it is usually possible to see moulds. Yeasts often **ferment** foods (break down the sugars in them to CO_2 gas and alcohol), so that the food tastes 'fizzy' and 'off'.

Food poisoning caused by bacteria can be very serious, and sometimes fatal. Some well-known food poisoning bacteria include *E. Coli* 0157, *Salmonella* and *Campylobacter*.

How can foods be kept safe?

There are some basic **food hygiene** rules that should be followed to reduce the risk of food poisoning:

- wash hands before handling food and after using the toilet or touching the nose
- do not cough, spit, sneeze or smoke near food
- wear clean clothes, and make sure nails are clean and hair is kept covered or tied back
- store foods correctly (see p112)
- keep foods and the kitchen clean
- use foods before they are past their date mark (see p71)
- keeps animals, flies, dust and rubbish away from foods
- use separate utensils to handle raw and cooked foods
- cook foods thoroughly and serve hot, or chill quickly if they are to be stored

Keeping the food industry safe

To help make sure that the food we eat is safe, the food industry has to follow certain rules and regulations. These rules are contained in the Food Safety Act 1990, which covers all aspects of food safety and aims to prevent the sale of food that is harmful to

One requirement of the Food Safety Act is the regular inspection of catering premises by an environmental health officer.

health. Anyone who has a business to do with food has to abide by this Act, and the Act is enforced by **environmental health officers** and **trading standards officers**, who are employed by local councils and authorities.

The Government has created a new agency called the Food Standards Agency, which has the power to monitor the safety and quality of food, from the start of food production until it reaches the consumer. It also offers advice and gives education on matters relating to food safety.

One way of ensuring food safety is to identify possible **risks** and **hazards** during the production, transport, storage and sale of food products. Food businesses are required to make a careful study of their buildings, workers and activities and work out where there are any possibilities for the food they deal with to become contaminated. This type of study is called a **Hazard Analysis of Critical Control Points** (**HACCP** for short). What does it mean?

Hazard Analysis = identifying the places, times or activities in the production process where the food could become unsafe

Critical Control Points = the points at which the food is at high risk of becoming unsafe, for example during storage, preparation or cooking

Workers in the food industry should ensure that all health and safety procedures are followed. Sometimes they don't!

HACCP is also used to check other aspects of food production, for example faults with packaging, unwanted items falling into a food product, or faulty mixing, cooking or chilling. Here is a HACCP for the production of plain set yogurt:

Stage of production	Potential problems	Solution
Workers	▸ poor personal hygiene (for example sneezing/coughing over food, dirty hands/nails)	▸ regular health checks for chest, nose, throat or digestive infections ▸ clean overalls daily, hair covered, white plastic boots and gloves worn (clean daily) ▸ no persons allowed in production room unless suitably dressed
Storage of milk	▸ milk residues could remain in tanks, storage temperature may rise if equipment is faulty	▸ tanks must be sterilized after each use ▸ storage temperature no more than 4 °C ▸ used on day of delivery
Storage of bacteria culture	▸ if not sealed properly, other bacteria may enter culture	▸ chilled in sealed container until required
Heating of milk	▸ if temperature is too low, harmful bacteria may multiply	▸ heated to 90 °C for 30 minutes to kill harmful bacteria in milk
Cooling of milk	▸ if the milk is cooled too slowly, the bacteria culture will not ferment the milk properly	▸ rapidly cooled to 44 °C
Addition of bacteria culture	▸ measurement of bacteria may not be carried out accurately	▸ the two types of bacteria must be in equal quantities to produce a good result
Incubation of yogurt	▸ if not incubated properly, the bacteria culture will not set the yogurt; if the seal is not tight, other micro-organisms will enter the yogurt	▸ at 44 °C for one-and-a-half hours, then poured into sterile pots until set (same temperature); pots covered and sealed
Cooling of product and storage	▸ if stored at higher temperature, bacteria will continue to multiply and spoil the yogurt	▸ cooled to 5–8 °C and stored at this temperature for no more than 14 days

QUESTIONS

1 Study the picture on the left, and list all the items and activities that could lead to food becoming unsafe to eat.
2 Find out what a Basic Food Hygiene Certificate is, who needs one and how they would obtain one.
3 Write a HACCP for any of the following:
   a) the delicatessen section of a supermarket selling cooked and raw meats, salads, prepared take-away curries and Chinese food, cheeses and pies
   b) a take-away burger bar
   c) a bakery selling fresh cream cakes, breads, sandwiches, etc.
   d) a soup kitchen providing hot soup and sandwiches for homeless people from a mobile kitchen

PROJECT **Keeping fit and healthy**

Brief

Recent research has shown that many school-age children may develop heart disease when they are adults because they eat too many fatty and sugary foods and do not take enough exercise. Design and produce a healthy food product that could be served as the main part of an evening meal, and would appeal to children at junior school.

A healthy food product is one that meets some or all of the requirements of healthy eating guidelines, i.e. that people should

- eat less fat
- eat less sugar
- eat less salt
- eat more fibre
- eat more starchy foods
- eat more fruit and vegetables

Research

- What is heart disease?
- Why are fatty and sugary foods bad for health?
- Which foods are fatty and sugary?
- Which foods are not fatty and sugary?
- Why is exercise good for the heart?

Excess weight puts a strain on various parts of the body and can lead to conditions such as heart disease and high blood pressure.

❖ Why are children taking less exercise?

❖ Why do children eat too many fatty and sugary foods?

❖ Read supermarket information leaflets, food labels and packets, books and magazines on health, fitness, food and nutrition, and PE, and information leaflets in health centres, doctors' surgeries and sports centres.

❖ Carry out a survey on the amount of exercise school children take in a week (for example, walking to school, swimming, football).

❖ Carry out a survey on the amount of fatty and sugary foods school children eat in a week.

❖ Design a questionnaire on the types of food school children like to eat for a main meal and ask children at your school to complete it.

Your specification

Write down what the product will be like:

▶ Will it be vegetarian or non-vegetarian?

▶ Will it be served hot or cold?

▶ What shape and size, colour and texture will it be?

▶ What ingredients will it contain and why will it be healthy?

▶ How will it be packaged?

▶ In which part of a supermarket will it be sold?

▶ How much will it cost?

▶ Why will children like it?

▶ How will it be kept safe to eat while it is being made and stored?

Your ideas

Use recipe books, leaflets and cards to find ideas. Write down your ideas and those of your friends (brainstorming). Choose two or three products to make. Think of a name for each product.

Develop your ideas

Make the product you have chosen. Set up a tasting panel and ask your friends to give your products scores on flavour, texture, colour and appeal. Choose one product. Use the results from the tasting panel to change or improve the product if necessary.

Make a final product specification

Find out how a similar food product would be made in industry, and how it would be packaged, labelled and sold in the shops.

Making and evaluating

Make the product and evaluate it to see whether it answers the brief and fits the specification.

PROJECT Snack foods

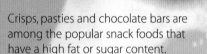

Crisps, pasties and chocolate bars are among the popular snack foods that have a high fat or sugar content.

Snack foods are eaten in large quantities in the UK and many other countries. People eat snack foods between or instead of meals every day, or at parties and picnics. Many snack-food products are designed to be eaten quickly and easily, and to be filling and satisfying.

There are several different categories (groups) of snack-food product, including:

▶ Bread-based snacks, for example sandwiches, baguettes (French bread sticks), tortillas and pitta bread, all of which can have different fillings.

▶ Pastry-based snacks, for example pies, flans, pasties, tarts, rolls and parcels, all of which can have different savoury or sweet fillings.

▶ Fried snacks, for example potato- or corn-based crisps, sticks, biscuits, or shaped snacks.

▶ Bars (usually sweet), for example cereal or chocolate bars, cakes, sponge rolls.

▶ Instant hot snacks, for example soups or noodle-based products to which the consumer adds boiling water.

A large number of snack-food products have fat and/or sugar as the main ingredients, for example chocolate and confectionery, fried potato and corn snacks (for example crisps, tortilla crisps), biscuits, cereal bars, ready-to-eat smoked sausages, pastry pies and pasties. Many of them are also highly seasoned with salt or artificial flavourings and often have colourings added.

Brief

A food manufacturer decides to produce a new range of snack foods targeted at people who want to follow a healthy lifestyle. Design and produce a savoury or sweet product from one of the categories of snack-food products that would suit the needs of this target group of people.

Research

❖ Identify the needs and wants of the people in this target group.
❖ List the images that a healthy lifestyle conjures up. Which could be used to identify and promote a snack-food product for this target group?
❖ Find out what the current advice for healthy food choices is.
❖ Identify suitable ingredients that could be used for this type of product.

A sandwich, a salad and an apple make a healthy alternative to the traditional snack lunch.

❖ Carry out a survey to find out what the most popular types of snack-food product in your chosen category are.
❖ Examine some existing snack-food products in your chosen category, and evaluate whether or not they meet current healthy eating guidelines. Look particularly at the amounts of sugar, fat and salt they contain (listed on the nutrition information panel on the labels). Comment on what you find out.
❖ Look at some existing 'healthy eating' versions of snack foods in your chosen category, and say how they have been adapted to make them 'healthy'.

Your specification

Write down what the product will be like:
▸ Will it be sweet or savoury?
▸ Will it be ready to eat or need the addition of, for example, boiling water?
▸ How will it meet the needs of healthy eating advice and lifestyles?
▸ How will it be packaged?
▸ How will it be promoted?
▸ How will it be stored in a shop?
▸ How will it be kept safe to eat during preparation, cooking, transport and storage?
▸ How much will it cost to make and buy?

Your ideas

Use recipe books, leaflets and cards to find ideas. Write down your ideas. Choose two or three products to make as prototypes (models). Think of a name for each product.

Develop your ideas

Make the products you have chosen and set up a tasting panel. Ask your friends to give your products scores on flavour, texture, colour and appeal. Choose one product. Use the results from the tasting panel to change or improve the product if necessary.

Unit 3 — Using ICT to support research and designing

By the end of this section, you should be able to:

- Understand how to organize and set out a project.
- Understand the importance of good presentation.
- Identify ways in which ICT can be used to research, design and present your work.

Organizing and presenting project work

What are projects for?

Projects are used to investigate, in detail, a topic or a problem so that it can be explained to other people and solved.

A good project should be presented:

- neatly, with easy-to-find sections and clearly labelled headings
- in a logical order (one that makes sense)
- in an interesting way, for example with pictures, charts and easy-to-read text, written in your own words

Who writes projects?

In addition to projects produced by school and college students, many projects are carried out by companies, for a variety of reasons, for example:

- to find out whether a new out-of-town supermarket is needed in an area
- to find out whether a crop can be grown in a certain area
- to find out why they are receiving complaints about a particular food packaging, and how it can be improved
- to find out whether consumers want a certain type of food product, for example ready-made meals

Organizing and setting out a project

General tips and ideas:

- For written projects, use a folder or binder to keep the pages secure, clean and crease-free.
- If you want to illustrate each page with a decorative border, clip art or photograph, you can save time in the following ways:
  - use a black-and-white design and photocopy it for the number of pages you need;
  - design a coloured border on the computer, save it and print copies as you need them;
  - scan or create a digital image on the computer, save it, and print copies as you need them.

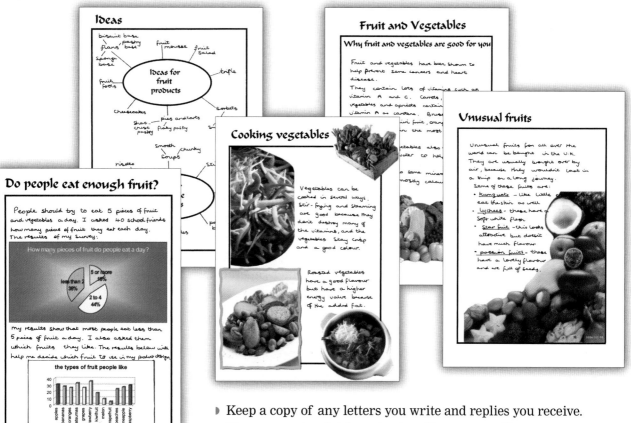

A good project should be clear and neat, and present information in a variety of ways.

▶ Keep a copy of any letters you write and replies you receive.

▶ Use a computer database to store the names, addresses, telephone numbers and references of any companies or organizations you have used to help you research a topic.

▶ Use a computer spreadsheet to present some of your data, the results of an experiment or survey, or to work out the costing for a new food product you have designed.

▶ Present a multimedia version of your project, using sound, moving images (for example animations and video clips), pictures and graphics to explain what you have found out.

▶ Don't forget to SAVE your work every time you use the computer, preferably on a floppy disk, so that you don't lose it!

There are many different ways of carrying out a project. This is a suggested order of work for a project in which a topic or problem is researched and a suitable food product is produced, but it could be adapted to suit different situations:

▶ **Contents page** This will be written last, once you know how many pages you have, and the order in which they will appear.

▶ **Introduction** Explain what you have been asked to do (the brief), and how you are going to do it.

▶ **Initial (first) ideas** Write down (brainstorm) your ideas about how you will carry out the project. These could be presented as a spider diagram.

▶ **Research** (see p46).

> **Initial ideas for food products** Write down your ideas for food products. You could describe and illustrate these using a computer modelling package.
> **Make a specification** for the type of food product you intend to produce (see p9).
> **Make** some of your food product ideas and evaluate them (see p10). Choose the best one. (You may be asked to produce more than one.)
> **Develop** your chosen food product, giving ideas as to how it could be improved or changed. You could use a spreadsheet to create a flow-chart that shows how your ideas have developed.
> **Write a final specification** for your chosen product.
> **Test** your chosen product on other people and write down their reactions to it and opinions about it. You could present the results as computer-generated graphs or pie charts.

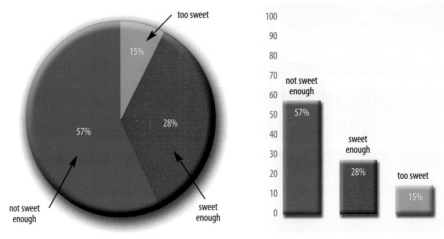

Test results shown as a pie chart   The same results as a bar graph

> Write about how you would keep the product **safe to eat** while it was being prepared, cooked, stored, packaged, delivered and sold (see p34).
> **Design packaging** for your product, showing how it would work and what information it would give (see p74). You could use computer-aided design (CAD) to do this.
> **Evaluate** your project, saying what you have found out, what you found easy or difficult, and how you could improve it another time.

QUESTIONS

1 When working on a project, why is it important to keep a copy of all the letters you write and receive?
2 What are the characteristics of a good project?
3 Think about a project you have done, and write down three ways in which it could have been improved.

Brief

A supermarket wants to produce a range of ready-made main meals from different countries. Choose one country and design and produce a suitable product that could be displayed in the chilled cabinet in a supermarket.

I am going to find out about different countries and the foods that are traditionally eaten every day and for special occasions. Because there are so many countries, I will choose a few from different areas of the world. I will then choose one country and try to design a product that will appeal to lots of different people.

Initial ideas

Areas of the world: Continental Europe, Central Europe and Russia, the Mediterranean, the Middle East, Africa, the Far East, North America, South America, Australia

Countries, traditional foods eaten and special occasions

	Continental Europe	
	FRANCE	ITALY
Countries		
Foods	Meats, pâtés, sausages, fresh fruit and vegetables, cheeses, croissants, baguettes, salads, garlic, snails, mussels	Pasta, tomatoes, mozzarella cheese, parmesan cheese, olives, olive oil, tuna, pizza, sardines, anchovies, rice, maize, citrus fruits, minestrone soup, lasagne, risotto, pasta and sauces
Special occasions	Bastille Day Mardi Gras	Carnival

	The Middle East	The Far East
Countries	SYRIA, IRAQ, SAUDI ARABIA, EGYPT, etc.	INDIA
Foods	Spices, fresh herbs, cereals (wheat & rice), beans, lamb, goat meat, figs, dates, citrus fruits, grapes, chick peas, lentils, vegetables, pitta bread, hummus, falafel, burghul (cracked wheat), goat or sheep's milk yogurt	rice, maize, millet, wheat, beans, lentils, spices, sugar, bananas, Nan bread, ghee, dhal, curries, chapatis, okra, aubergines
Special occasions	Muslim – Meelad-al-Nabil, Ramadan Id-ul-Azha No pork or alcohol Halal meat	Hindu – Holi, Raksha Bandha, Janam Ashtami, Dussehra, Divali Many vegetarians – no meat, eggs, fish. Cow is sacred – milk products eaten

Initial ideas for food products

Chosen country – India   Type of food product – Curries

I have chosen curries because they have become very popular in the UK since they have been available in Indian restaurants and take-aways. In India, people don't use the word 'curry' but people in this country know what it means, so I will use it. Traditionally, curries are made by preparing spices (crushing, chopping, grating) and mixing these with other ingredients and leaving the mixture to marinade for a few hours. This lets the flavour into the other ingredients. I think people don't have enough time to do this, but want to eat a traditional curry, so my products would be made with fresh spices and herbs to make them taste as authentic as possible.

Ideas:

Lamb and bean curry – mild flavour
Vegetarian curry – medium flavour
Chicken and fruit curry – hot flavour

Unit 3

Carrying out research

By the end of this section, you should be able to:

▶ Understand why research is important.
▶ Identify different places to find out information.
▶ Identify how ICT can help you to research a topic.
▶ Understand how to present your research.

Food magazines, leaflets and websites produced by retailers provide useful information on a variety of subjects.

Why do research?

Research involves making a careful investigation of something to find out new facts and information about it. In food technology, you might be asked to investigate a number of different topics, for example a new food product; what someone can eat if they have a particular health need; how you can reduce the amount of sugar in a food product; or how you can make a product attractive to people. Research is a very important part of food product development (see p8).

Food technology research can be carried out in different ways:
▶ reading about a topic to find out facts
▶ investigating and comparing food products
▶ doing experiments with foods and recipes
▶ asking people questions and their opinions

Finding out facts

There are a number of places to find out facts, including:
▶ books, magazines, newspapers and food journals (your local library can help)
▶ Internet websites and computer programs, for example encyclopaedias, nutritional analysis programs
▶ writing to food manufacturers, retailers, caterers, government organizations, food industry organizations, healthcare trusts, consumer and health organizations
▶ many companies use computer-mediated communications (CMC) such as websites and e-mail to give information to consumers and answer questions about their products and services, which may be a quicker way of collecting information
▶ food labels and packaging, and information leaflets produced by retailers and food manufacturers
▶ television and radio programmes

Useful tips:
▶ Don't copy chunks of information from books or the computer; make sure that you understand the information, then write it in your own words.
▶ When searching for information on the Internet, try to give a specific description of what you are looking for, otherwise you may end up with hundreds of websites to look at, many of which will not be relevant to your project.

▶ When writing away for information, be as specific as you can about the information you want; this will help the person at the other end to understand exactly what information you need and why you need it.

Investigating food products

Looking at and comparing food products can give you some useful information. Here are some ideas of what to look for and investigate:

▶ **information on the label or packaging**, for example ingredients, nutritional value, additives used, weight or volume, where it was made, storing, preparation, cooking and serving instructions, suitability for different people

▶ **the cost compared with similar products**, per item or per 100 g or 100 ml (supermarkets often show this on the shelf where the product is displayed)

▶ **the packaging** – how it is made, what it looks like, how well it protects the food, how easy it is to use

▶ **the flavour, colour, texture, smell** of foods before and after they are cooked or frozen

▶ **what it is made of** – some products, for example dried soups, muesli, pies, pasties, ready meals, fruit cake, cereal bars, can be taken apart (**disassembled**) to find out what they contain. The individual parts can either be counted (for example pieces of meat or vegetable in a soup or ready meal, glacé cherries in a fruit cake, nuts and dried fruit in muesli) or weighed (e.g. pastry in a pie, pie filling, fish in a fish finger, or pasta in a dried soup). This may show that some products are better quality or value for money than others.

By dissassembling (taking apart) a food product such as muesli we can see what it is made of and how much of each ingredient it contains.

Experimenting with foods and recipes

There are a number of basic recipes (for example for sauces, cakes, biscuits, soups, breads, pastries, cold and hot puddings), that can be adapted (changed) to suit different needs by using different amounts or types of ingredients. Adapting recipes is important in new food product development. Many food manufacturers have a recipe development kitchen, where people are employed to experiment with foods as part of the design process when a new product is being developed. Sometimes they will develop a set of recipes using a food product to show consumers how versatile (useful for a variety of different occasions) the product is. These may be printed on the packaging or offered as a recipe booklet.

Recipes can be adapted in many ways:

▶ the amount of sugar in cake, pudding and biscuit recipes can be reduced
▶ the amount or type of fat in cake, pastry, sauce and biscuit recipes can be reduced or changed
▶ the amount of fibre in bread, cake and biscuit recipes can be increased by adding bran or using wholemeal flour in different amounts
▶ salt can be left out of savoury recipes and other flavours, for example herbs and spices, can be used instead
▶ different methods of cooking, for example grilling instead of frying, steaming vegetables instead of boiling them
▶ fruit can be added to a savoury recipe
▶ fruit and/or nuts can be added to breads, cakes and biscuits
▶ foods can be combined in unusual ways for sandwich or jacket potato fillings or pizza toppings, for example fresh fruit with meat or cheese, or beans with curry spices

Recipes can be adapted to suit different requirements by adding or removing ingredients.

QUESTIONS

1 Collect some food labels, for example breakfast cereals, ready-made meals, canned fish and pasta, and write down what you can find out about the product from the information on the label. Say whether or not you found the information easy to read and understand, and how you think it could be improved.
2 Collect some information leaflets about food and nutrition from supermarkets and read them. Write down what you think about:
  ▶ the way the information on them is presented
  ▶ whether or not the information is easy to read and understand
  ▶ what ICT skills were used to put the information together and present it
  ▶ what types of information are the most interesting and useful
3 Find a page of information about a food topic in a book or encyclopaedia, or on a website, for example about bread, cheese-making, healthy eating or frozen foods. Read the information and then write it out in your own words. Present it as an information leaflet that could be given to your friends, to help explain the topic to them.

PROJECT Foods from around the world

Mexico · The Caribbean · West Africa · Japan

West Africa

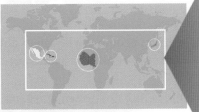

Cereal plants such as millet are important in Africa because they grow very quickly in areas of drought.

Cassava tubers are cooked and then pounded to make a type of porridge called *fufu*.

West Africa covers a large area of Africa and includes countries such as Cameroon, Nigeria, Ghana and Mali. Most people in these countries live in villages, and many of them grow their own food, but there are also several large cities, for example Lagos in Nigeria and Timbuktu in Mali.

The climate in West Africa is tropical. There is a wet and a dry season, but it is hot all year round. Some parts of the land are very fertile (plants grow well in the soil) with lush vegetation, and some areas are less fertile and more like a desert.

The list below shows the types of food grown in West Africa. It is important to remember that many people in this area of the world are poor and cannot afford to buy these foods. Many of the crops they grow are exported to richer countries like the UK, and the farmers who grow them do not make much money from them.

- **citrus fruits** — oranges, grapefruit, limes
- A variety of other **fruits**, for example bananas, pineapples, pawpaws, mangoes, coconuts
- **maize** and **millet** are pounded into flour and used to make porridge and cakes
- **cassava** are pressed and dried, then pounded to make *fufu*, a type of porridge
- **groundnuts** (peanuts) often made into stew with chicken and vegetables
- **plantains** and **yams** are also made into *fufu*; yams are also boiled and served with meat or fish
- some **rice** is grown but is expensive to buy
- some **cattle** are reared for meat
- **chickens** are kept and used for meat and eggs
- **fish** are caught from the sea and rivers
- imported **wheat** is made into bread
- many other foods are **imported**

PROJECT

Mexico

Mexico is a large country situated at the southern end of North America. It has several different regions, including deserts, cold mountain regions and humid rainforests. Over two-thirds of the population live in towns and cities.

The first people to live in Mexico were Indians. The Spanish conquered the country in the 16th century, bringing with them not only the Spanish language, which most Mexicans now speak, but also lots of new foods.

The list below shows some of the foods that are grown and eaten in Mexico. Many of the people are poor, and cannot afford to buy all the foods on the list.

▶ **maize** (corn) — the most important crop for thousands of years; there are hundreds of recipes using maize, the most well known being tortillas (made from maize flour) and tacos
▶ **wheat** — made into breads, pastries, cakes and burritos (a wheat tortilla filled with rice, beans and meat and chilli sauce)
▶ **cacao beans** — from which chocolate is made
▶ a variety of **fruits**, for example papayas, watermelons, citrus fruits, pineapples, avocados, mangoes, bananas
▶ a variety of **vegetables**, for example, peppers, custard marrows, cactus plants, potatoes, beans, chillies (about 100 varieties) often used to make salsa dips and added to meat and fish dishes
▶ **pork** and **beef** — the most popular meats eaten; pork sausages called chorizos are also popular
▶ **chicken** and **turkey**
▶ **goat** and **mutton** — often eaten in a spicy sauce
▶ **dairy foods**, for example cheeses and milk (often blended with fruit and cereal to make a drink called a smoothie)
▶ **seafoods**, for example prawns and octopus

Cactuses grow in the dry desert regions of northern Mexico.

The Caribbean

The Caribbean Islands are situated in the Caribbean Sea, between North and South America. There are thousands of islands, some of the more well known ones being Jamaica, Cuba, Barbados, St Lucia and Trinidad. The islands mostly have a hot, tropical climate, with a rainy and a hurricane season.

Between 500 and 300 years ago, many of the islands were invaded and colonized by European countries, including Britain, France, Spain and The Netherlands. Many sugar cane plantations were set up, using African slaves to work on them, and the sugar was exported to Europe.

Today, many crops are grown in the Caribbean because the climate is so warm. Many of the foods eaten in the Caribbean were introduced from other countries, such as Africa.

The list below shows some of the foods that are grown and eaten in the Caribbean. Many people are poor and cannot afford to buy these foods, which are usually exported for cash.

- **vegetables**, for example cassava, sweet potatoes, yams, eddoes (cocoyams), callaloo (like spinach)
- **fruits**, for example bananas (now a major export crop), mangoes, coconuts, oranges, avocados, limes, breadfruit, ackee, plantains, papayas (pawpaws), guavas
- **spices**, for example nutmeg, mace (curries are very popular)
- **sugar cane**
- **coffee**
- **rice** — often made into a dish called rice and peas, where the peas are actually different types of beans
- **fish** and **seafood**
- **pork, chicken, beef** (often coated in a spicy sauce and barbecued — a traditional dish called Jerk chicken, pork or beef)
- **wheat flour** and other **cereals** are imported

Bananas are exported from the Caribbean.

About 5 million people were taken from West Africa to work as slaves on the sugar plantations of the Caribbean.

Seafood, barbecued meat and fresh fruit and vegetables are some of the foods eaten in the Caribbean.

PROJECT

Japan

Japan is situated on the far-eastern side of Asia, near China. It has four main islands and nearly 4,000 small islands. Even though it occupies one of the world's smallest areas of land, it has one of the largest populations. Most people live in crowded cities.

Some parts of Japan have a semi-tropical climate; others are like northern Europe, with four definite seasons. Every available piece of land is used for growing crops such as rice and vegetables.

Many traditional foods are eaten in Japan, but 'Western' fast foods such as pizzas and burgers are becoming very popular. The list below shows some of the foods that are grown and eaten in Japan. Rice is the staple food eaten by most people.

- **rice** – grown in paddy fields
- **fruits**, for example mandarin oranges, grapes, peaches, plums, pears, apples
- **vegetables**, for example spinach, potatoes, sweet potatoes, *taro* (like yams), mushrooms (various types), aubergines, Chinese cabbage, white radishes, seaweed
- **tea**
- **fish** and **seafood** — a large variety; saltwater and freshwater fish, eels and seafood are often grown on fish farms
- **meat** and **dairy foods** are eaten in smaller amounts, but as more foods are imported, they are becoming popular
- **Soya beans** (often imported) made into soy sauce, miso (a salty paste), tofu (soya bean curd), and natto (a breakfast food)

Three-quarters of Japanese people live in or near towns and cities.

Like all cereal plants, rice is a type of grass.

Japanese sushi restaurants have become popular in the West.

Brief

Investigate the foods commonly grown and eaten in a country of your choice. Then design a range of food products (for example, ready-made meals, pastries, breads) that a food manufacturer could produce to promote the foods from that region. Make one of the products.

Research

- Find out how some of the food products you are investigating became popular in your chosen country. Use the Internet, encyclopaedias or books for your research. At the library, a subject search computer program will help you to find suitable books.
- Find out which foods from your chosen country are imported and available to buy in the UK.
- Find out about the food value of these foods, using a nutritional analysis program on a computer or food tables.
- Carry out a survey to find out whether people know about foods from your chosen country, and show them pictures of, for example, fruits and vegetables to see whether they can identify them.
- Use a computer to design a quiz sheet, to see whether people can identify the foods, and put it in your project. Present your results as computer-generated graphs or pie charts.
- Suggest ways in which a manufacturer and food retailer could promote foods from your chosen country.
- Design your own promotional materials using a computer art program, or draw your own, scan them, and produce promotional leaflets, labels, or posters.
- Find out about festivals and traditions involving foods from your chosen country.
- You might be able to e-mail a food company in the country you have chosen, and ask them questions about the foods.

Your specification

Write about what your product will be like:
- Who will be the target group for your product?
- Will it be vegetarian or non-vegetarian?
- How will it be packaged and labelled?
- How will you attract people to buy it?
- How will it be kept safe and fit to eat during preparation, cooking, transport and storage?

PROJECT Sports drinks

When people take an active part in sports, they have to make sure that they look after their bodies by having enough food and fluid. Sports that involve lots of sprinting, such as rugby, football, squash, tennis and hockey, use lots of energy in short bursts, which must be supplied by a regular amount of food.

Endurance sports, such as marathon and track running, long-distance cycling and swimming also use large amounts of energy, and people who do these sports have to make sure that they have a regular supply of high-energy, nutritionally balanced food to keep their bodies in peak condition.

Probably the most important factor in maintaining exercise performance is replacing the large amounts of fluid that are lost from the body in sweat. Sweating is the body's natural mechanism for cooling itself down during exercise.

During prolonged exercise, the body can lose between 1 and 2 litres of sweat per hour. Sweat contains water and important salts that are needed by the body for maintaining the correct concentration of all body fluids. If large amounts of sweat are lost, the body can suffer with severe muscle cramps and dehydration.

Liquid energy

In the last few years, a variety of sports drinks have been designed and developed by food manufacturers. Many claim to replace lost body fluid more quickly than water and to replace the body salts.

Some are described as 'isotonic'. This means that they contain some glucose as well as salts, to provide energy. It is known that isotonic fluid is absorbed more quickly by the body than plain water, so this is why manufacturers use this description.

Isotonic sports drinks, which contain glucose and salts, are quickly absorbed by the body.

If sports drinks contain too much glucose or sugar, they can become sticky and messy if spilled whilst a runner is drinking them, and can also allow bacteria to grow in them in warm temperatures if they are not sealed properly.

Carbonated (fizzy) drinks are not suitable, as they would bubble out of a container if shaken whilst running, and would also cause discomfort in the stomach as the CO_2 gas they contain tries to escape.

Increased fluid intake is essential in order to avoid dehydration during sporting activities such as long-distance cycling and running.

Brief

Design and make a sports drink suitable for being sold from a vending machine in a local sports centre, where a variety of sports are played. The drink should provide energy and contain natural ingredients. Design some alternative flavours to produce a range of drinks.

Research

❖ What are the most popular flavours?
❖ What types of natural ingredient could be used?
❖ What would be the best method of producing the drink?
❖ What would be the best way of packaging the drink?
❖ What information would the label on the drink need to show?

Your specification

▸ What are the ingredients in your product?
▸ What flavour range will you produce?
▸ How much will the product cost?
▸ Who is your target group?
▸ How will the drink be kept safe during production, storage and distribution?
▸ How will you promote your product?

Unit (4) Exploring ingredients

A varied diet is important because different foods contain different nutrients.

Nutrition

Why do we need food?

We need to eat food several times every day. This is because we need food to make us **grow**, keep us **healthy**, and give us **energy**. A **mixture** of foods will give us all the things we need. Eating food makes us feel good, and eating together with other people is an important **social** (friendly) activity.

What is food?

Food comes from plants and animals, and can be either liquid or solid.

Food has different flavours, colours, odours (smells) and textures, and contains **nutrients** and water.

What are nutrients?

Nutrients are special substances that do different jobs in the body. Some foods contain several different nutrients; some foods have only one or two. It is important to eat a mixture of foods every day, in order to get all the nutrients.

Nutrient	Job in the body	Found mostly in these foods
Protein	Makes the body grow. Repairs the body when it is injured. Gives the body some energy.	peas, beans (especially soya), wheat, rice, oats, lentils, Quorn, meat, fish, cheese, eggs, milk
Fat	Gives the body lots of energy. Can be used to store energy in the body. Helps to keep the body warm.	liquid oils: vegetable oils e.g. olive, sunflower, maize, nuts; fish liver oils, e.g. cod liver oil solid fats: butter, lard, suet, margarine, white vegetable fats, cream, cheese hidden fats: pastry, potato chips and crisps, fried snacks, meat, sausages, nuts, cakes, biscuits, chocolate, mayonnaise, salad dressings, sausages
Carbohydrate	Gives the body lots of energy.	all sugars e.g. sucrose (sugar used in cooking), fructose (sugar found in fruit), lactose (sugar found in milk), glucose (sugar found in ripe fruits and vegetables), maltose (sugar found in cereals); starch in fruits and vegetables, cornflour, wheat

		flour, pasta, and cereals; hidden sugars in sweets, chocolate, biscuits, cakes, many sauces, canned fruits and vegetables, soft drinks, snack foods

Vitamins

Vitamin A	Helps the eyes to see in dim light. Helps to keep the throat, lungs and digestive system moist and healthy. Helps to keep the skin healthy. Helps children to grow.	carrots, green leafy vegetables, apricots, tomatoes, sweetcorn, milk, cheese, egg yolk, butter, oily fish, cod liver oil, liver
Vitamin B group (there are several B vitamins)	Helps the body to get energy from food. Helps the body to grow. Helps the nerves and muscles to work properly. Helps blood to be made properly. Helps to keep the skin healthy. Helps to keep the digestive system, lungs, and mouth moist and healthy.	wholegrain cereals, bread, yeast, yeast extract, milk, meat, eggs
Vitamin C	Helps to keep the skin, blood vessels, gums and all the cells of the body healthy and joined together. Helps the body to absorb (take in) iron from food. Helps to make the bones and teeth strong. Helps to prevent heart disease.	blackcurrants, oranges, lemons, limes, grapefruit, satsumas, kiwi fruit, peppers, strawberries, broccoli, Brussels sprouts, cabbage, beansprouts, peas, potatoes
Vitamin D (made under the skin by sunlight)	Makes bones and teeth grow strong and healthy. Helps the body absorb (take in) calcium and phosphorus from food.	liver, cod liver oil, oily fish, margarine, milk, butter, egg yolk
Vitamin E	Helps to lower the risk of heart disease.	lettuce, cereals, peanuts, egg yolk, seeds, wheatgerm oil, vegetable oils, milk

Minerals

There are lots of different minerals that are needed by the body. Some of them are listed below.

Calcium	Makes bones and teeth strong. Helps make the blood clot after an injury. Helps keep the muscles and nerves healthy.	green leafy vegetables, milk, cheese, yogurt, bread, bones of canned fish, cereals
Phosphorus	Works with calcium to make strong bones and teeth. Helps the body to get energy from food.	all natural plant and animal foods
Iron	Makes red blood cells, which carry oxygen around the body.	liver, kidney, green leafy vegetables, curry powder, cocoa, chocolate, dried fruit, lentils, white bread, wholegrain cereals
Fluoride	Helps to make the enamel (outer layer) of teeth strong.	tea, sea-water fish, some tap water

Food contains two more things that do important jobs in the body:

Water	Our bodies are 70% water. We cannot live without water for more than a few days.	drinking water, fruits, vegetables, milk

	Water is needed for all body fluids and actions, e.g. digesting food, moving, getting rid of waste from the body.	
Dietary fibre (non-starch polysaccharides or NSP)	Helps the body to get rid of waste products by making the faeces (solid waste products) soft and bulky. Helps prevent constipation and other diseases in the intestines, such as cancer.	wholegrain rice, oats, wholemeal bread and pasta, bran, fruit, vegetables, high-fibre breakfast cereals

The diet of a pregnant woman should provide her body with enough nutrients to cope with the demands of the growing baby as well as its own needs.

It is important to eat a **balanced diet** (a mixture of foods) to give your body the right amount of nutrients. People who do not have enough food, and therefore not enough nutrients to make the body grow, stay healthy, and have energy may suffer from **under-nutrition**. People who have too much or too little of a particular nutrient may suffer from **malnutrition**. This may result in poor health, for example, too much fat may make the body overweight; too little calcium will make the bones and teeth weak.

How much should we eat?

The amount of food you need depends on:
▶ Your **age**.
▶ How **active** you are.
▶ Whether you are **male or female**.
▶ What **condition** your body is in, for example, pregnant, breast-feeding, recovering from an illness, accident or operation, building up strength to take part in sport.

Different needs

Look at the charts on the page opposite. They show how the body needs different amounts of nutrients and energy at different stages of life. The information used in the charts is for *most* people in the population. It is important to remember that some people need more and some people need less of a nutrient than is shown on the charts. For example, someone in a very active job, such as a footballer, will use more energy than someone sitting at a desk in an office, and a tall teenager will need more calcium to grow their bones than a shorter teenager.

Sports people need both strength and stamina.

A person's nutritional requirements change with age.

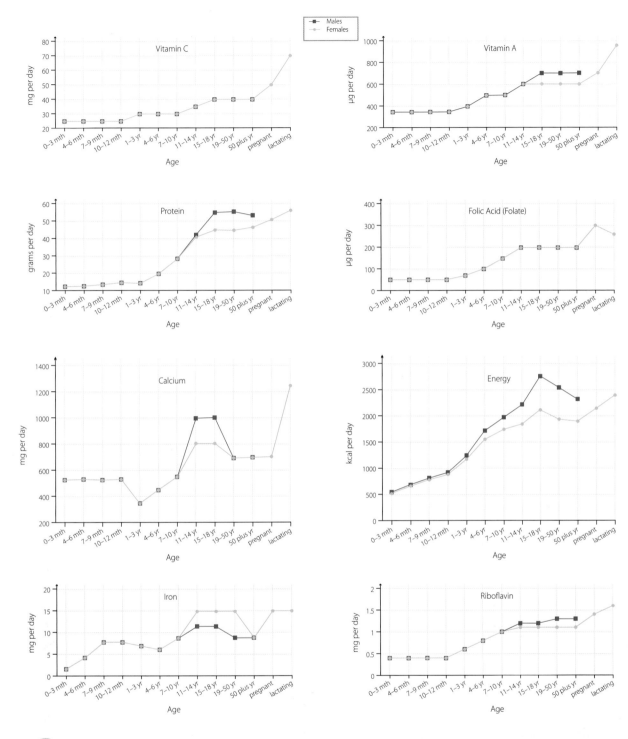

QUESTIONS

1 How do food manufacturers tell people which nutrients are found in their products?

2 What types of food product do manufacturers produce to help people eat healthily?

3 Why do children, teenagers and pregnant women need plenty of protein and calcium in their food?

4 Why do foods such as milk and eggs have several different nutrients in them?

5 Find out what types of food athletes and other sports men and women eat to give them energy. Which food products have a sporty image?

Unit Presenting food products

Choosing food

There are a number of factors that affect our choice of food, for example:

- cost
- what there is available to choose from
- likes and dislikes
- beliefs, traditions and customs
- familiarity (knowing what a food is and what it should taste like)
- advertising
- the opinions of other people
- fashion and trends
- health and well-being
- appearance and presentation

Look at the two pictures below, which show the same food product served in different ways. Which one appeals to you most? Why?

There is no doubt that the appearance and presentation of food will affect whether or not people choose to eat it. People have expectations about the colour, shape and texture of foods, which influence their choices. It does not matter if a food product tastes wonderful — if it is poorly presented, it is unlikely to be tasted.

Although the enjoyment of food involves all the senses — sight, smell, taste, touch and hearing — there is no doubt that sight has

Even the tastiest meal will seem unappetizing if poorly presented.

Attractive presentation makes a good first impression.

Advertisements are carefully designed to make the product appear attractive and appetizing.

the first and strongest influence. Food manufacturers and retailers recognize this fact, and spend large sums of money every year perfecting the appearance of their products in order to ensure that they sell. They do this by:

◗ careful photography of food products, showing them at their best, often with other foods
◗ designing suitable, attractive packaging
◗ careful use of colour and shape in products and in advertising
◗ attractive visual displays of a product

Food producers in restaurants and canteens are also aware of the importance of appearance, and try to produce food that is:

◗ served in clean, undamaged dishes and plates
◗ served in a neat and tidy way
◗ garnished and decorated to make the food look attractive
◗ served in clean and neat surroundings in which colour and light play a part in making the food look attractive

QUESTIONS

1　Why is the appearance and presentation of food so important?
2　Look at some advertisements for food products. Describe how the manufacturer or retailer has tried to make the food look attractive.
3　What difficulties might there be in taking colour photographs of the following foods for an advertisement or magazine article?
　　◗ ice cream
　　◗ vegetable soup
　　◗ a white wedding cake with pale-coloured flowers
　　◗ a hot meal, for example chicken pie, vegetables and gravy
　　◗ sponge pudding with hot custard
　　How might the photographer get round any difficulties?

PROJECT Feeding pre-school children

Meals for pre-school children should give them energy and provide nutrients for body growth.

Pre-school children are generally very active, inquisitive, and eager to learn and try new experiences. Their bodies grow at a fast rate, and they need to eat a good mixture of foods to give them:

▶ energy
▶ protein for growth
▶ calcium and vitamin D for the growth of bones and teeth
▶ fluoride to strengthen growing teeth
▶ iron for healthy blood
▶ other vitamins and minerals to keep them healthy and encourage growth, activity and the development of skills and abilities

Bad eating habits, such as eating a lot of sweets, salty and fatty snack foods and sugary drinks, can start at this age and may be difficult to break when they are older. Healthy eating advice for this age group has to be given to parents and carers who buy the food for the child, and taught to the child in a number of situations, for example in playgroups and nurseries, health care centres and parent and toddler groups. Food preparation sessions and mealtimes can be a good opportunity for teaching children about different foods, for example:

▶ where they come from
▶ how they grow
▶ what they contain
▶ what colours, flavours, textures and smells they have
▶ how they help the body to grow and stay healthy
▶ how they are prepared and cooked
▶ how they can be made interesting to eat and what you can eat them with

Many food products are aimed at pre-school children, and research has shown that even at this age, children take notice of brand names, and can easily identify foods from their logos. Pre-school children generally pay a lot of attention to advertisements, especially those shown on the television. In some countries, no advertising is allowed on television during children's viewing time. In the UK, advertisements for foods (many of which contain a lot of sugar, fat and salt) are shown during children's television time, and many are aimed at pre-school children.

Many food products are sold in brightly coloured packaging, with free toys or novelties, in order to appeal to pre-school children.

Brief

A food manufacturer wants to produce a range of ready-meals for pre-school children that can be stored in the chiller cabinet in a shop. The target groups are the parents and carers of this age group, who would find such products convenient.

The manufacturer wants the specifications of such products to follow current healthy eating advice for this age group, and also wants to keep additives to a minimum. Design a range of meals that would be suitable, and prepare and cook some examples of these.

Research

- What are the needs and wants of the target group of buyers and consumers of these products?
- What is the current healthy eating advice for pre-school children?
- How do food manufacturers target this age group and their parents/carers?
- What are the particular health and safety rules to be followed when preparing foods for this age group?
- What sort of information would the buyers of such products like to see on the labels of such products?
- How can children be encouraged to try different foods?

Your specifications

- Will any of your products be vegetarian?
- How will your products be prepared and cooked?
- How will your products be packaged?
- What flavours, textures and colours will your products contain?
- How will your products be labelled?
- What portion sizes will your products be?
- How will your products be kept safe to eat during preparation, cooking, packaging, transport, display and storage?

PROJECT Rice

Rice is the seeds (grains) from a cereal plant. All cereals are types of grass. After wheat, rice is the cereal most often eaten by people throughout the world. There are many different types of rice and rice products, for example:

Rice	Rice products
long-grain patna	breakfast cereals
basmati	rice cakes
Thai fragrant	ground rice (rice flour)
risotto	flaked rice
wild	rice noodles
Carolina	

Rice is an important and fairly inexpensive source of energy, protein, B vitamins and fibre. White rice has had the outer layers of each seed removed and cooks more quickly than brown rice. Brown or wholegrain rice has not had anything removed and contains more vitamins and fibre than white rice.

Rice is usually boiled in water and served with meat, fish and/or vegetables and sauces. It can also be used in meat or vegetable rissoles, fish cakes, meatballs, soups, stews and pasties. Some types of rice are used to make sweet puddings, biscuits and cakes.

Most rice is grown in swampy areas known as paddies.

There are more than 7000 varieties of rice, ranging from short grain to long grain. Some types of rice are used to make products such as flour, rice cakes and breakfast cereals.

Briefs

Choose one of the following:

1. In the army, when soldiers are on manoeuvres, they have to carry their food and cook it over a fire in the open air. Their food, matches and other items are usually packed in sealed cans or plastic packs to keep everything dry and undamaged. Design a savoury and a sweet rice-based meal that could be stored in a can and eaten hot or cold. Each can would hold enough for one person.

2. Vegans are people who don't eat any animal food or food product. They eat plant foods and food products such as cereals, fruit and vegetables, nuts, pulses and beans such as soya. Design a main course meal based on rice that would provide enough protein, calcium and iron for a teenage vegan.

3. People who have coeliac disease cannot eat a protein called **gluten**, which is found in wheat, barley, rye and oats, but not in rice or maize. Investigate this disease, and design a selection of biscuit (savoury and sweet), cake or pudding products using rice and maize that would appeal to children with coeliac disease.

4. The school canteen is trying to save money, but still provide pupils with interesting, filling and nutritious meals. Design a selection of savoury and sweet products based on rice that would meet these requirements and be suitable for producing on a large scale.

Research

❖ What are the particular needs of the target group in the brief you have chosen?
❖ If appropriate, conduct a survey to find out what kinds of rice products people prefer.

Your specification

Write down what your products will be like:

▸ How much would you serve in one portion?
▸ What would your products cost to make and sell per portion?
▸ How would each product be prepared, served and packaged?
▸ How would each product be kept appetizing and safe to eat during preparation, cooking and serving?

Unit ⑤ Designing for clients

Equipment used in food production

By the end of this section, you should be able to:
▶ Identify and compare types of equipment used in the home and in industry for the production of food.
▶ Identify the main points to consider when choosing suitable equipment for food production.

Wherever food products are made, they will be much easier to produce if suitable equipment is used. When food products are made on a **large scale**, as in factories, special equipment and machinery is designed to carry out particular **processes**, for example, cutting, mixing, sieving, heating, chilling, packaging. Often, computers control these processes. This is called **computer-aided manufacture (CAM)**. The computers are programmed to control or detect things such as:
▶ cooking temperature and time
▶ changes in weight or temperature
▶ the speed the products move along a conveyor belt
▶ the amount of flavouring added to a product, for example crisps

Information is constantly sent back to a control centre, where any necessary adjustments to the production of the food product will be made.

Successful food production on a large scale depends on:
▶ careful control of each stage of production
▶ regular inspection and maintenance of equipment
▶ well-trained operators

Computers can be used to monitor food production.

In large factories, the speed of conveyor belts is usually controlled by computer.

Look at the pictures showing different processes in food production being carried out. Notice the size of the equipment, how it is set out, the number of people needed to operate it, what they are wearing, and what the equipment is made of.

Equipment used to produce food on a **small scale**, as in the home and smaller catering kitchens, carry out a variety of processes. Many are operated by modern technology, for example microwave ovens, conventional cookers and food processors.

Successful food production on a small scale depends on:

- the skills of the people preparing and cooking the food
- the ability to use equipment confidently, safely and efficiently
- having knowledge and understanding of how different foods react when they are prepared and cooked

Look at the picture of the kitchen used for food production on a small scale. Notice the size of the equipment and where it is placed in the kitchen.

A well-planned, well-equipped kitchen is easy to work in.

Choosing suitable equipment

Here are some general guidelines for choosing equipment. These apply to all food production, however large- or small-scale it is.

- Choose the best affordable quality.
- Choose items that are easy and safe to operate.
- Choose items that can be used for a variety of processes, if possible.
- Choose equipment that can be cleaned easily and thoroughly.
- Choose items that come with a manufacturer's guarantee and are designed and made to a high safety standard.

The symbols of the BSI (British Standards Institution), left, and the British Electrotechnical Approvals Board, above left, assure consumers that goods have met certain safety requirements.

QUESTIONS

1 Using the guidelines for choosing equipment, make a list of what you would look for when choosing the following pieces of equipment:
   a) a frying pan
   b) a cook's knife
   c) an electric whisk
   d) a food processor
   e) a cooker
   f) a microwave oven
   Give reasons for your answers.

2 Find out why the following are suitable materials for making these pieces of equipment:
   a) wood for spoons used to stir hot liquids in pans
   b) stainless steel for pans
   c) stainless steel for worktops and sinks in a restaurant kitchen
   d) plastic and heat-proof glass containers for microwave ovens

3 Find out why the following might be needed in a large-scale food production factory:
   a) metal detectors and X-ray machines
   b) hair protectors and plastic gloves for operators
   c) air extractors and air conditioners

PROJECT Adapting food products

Briefs

Choose one of the following:

1. A restaurant in the centre of a large shopping area in a town is trying to change its image to attract families to eat there during the daytime. The restaurant wants to offer a variety of two- and three-course meals that can be enjoyed by all age groups. Explain how the restaurant can adapt the following to meet the needs of all age groups:

   ‣ its facilities (seating areas, toilets, entertainment)
   ‣ its menus (meal types and portions, menu designs)

   Prepare a main meal for a family of two adults and two pre-school children. Explain how the meal could be batch-produced (see page 84) and stored so that there is always a supply available to meet demand.

Some restaurants have separate dining and playing areas so that adults can relax while their children entertain themselves.

Restaurants that cater for families might have separate menus for adults and children.

Starters

...m Baked Open Cup Mushrooms
...ratatouille V or stilton and bacon   £3.75

...m Cocktail
...reat British favourite"   £3.75

...Famous Mixed Dippers (for two to sha...
...ed mushrooms, stuffed potato sh...
...red whole onion rings, ...

Breaded Ginger & Garlic P...
with a sweet chilli dip

Crispy Stuffed Potato She...
with ratatouille or cheese and ba...

Fresh Honeydew Melon V

Crispy Chicken Strips
on a bed of salad leaves with honey &...

Duck & Orange Pate
with toasted rustic bread and red onion...

Breaded Deep Fried Mushrooms
with a ranch dressing dip

Fresh Soup of the Day V
served with rustic bread

Dip Selection
V ranch dressing V thousand island V honey & ...

From the Grill

...ater we've always been famous for our o...
...ve that we provide fresh and ...
...quality. It is there...
...et exactl...

Choose your own favourite main course and pudding
plus a free drink and refill and we'll even give you a
chocolate treat to take home too!

£4.99

Over 5's
Drinks - Pepsi, Diet Pepsi, lemonade
(half pint draught servings only) and orange squash

Beef Burger with
chips and tomato
relish or mayonnaise
vegetarian burger
also available

Beefeater Fish and
Chips* with tartare
sauce and peas

Jumbo Yorkshire
Pudding filled with
prime pork sausages
peas and gravy or baked
beans with chips

Gammon Steak
and Pineapple
with chips and peas

2. A food manufacturer wants to adapt its current range of ready-made meals to meet the needs of people who want to follow healthy eating advice. Design and prepare two such products. Explain how they have been adapted to meet these needs and how they would be batch-produced.

3. A senior citizens' nursing home has a number of residents who are diabetic. The chef has been asked to adapt the meals of the diabetic patients without making them feel too different from the other residents. Design three two-course dinners for the home, showing how they can be adapted for the diabetics. Prepare one of the meals.

4. A biscuit manufacturer wants to adapt one of its popular products to offer consumers some alternative flavours and textures. The current product is flavoured with vanilla. Design biscuits with alternative flavours and textures and make some of your designs. Explain how the manufacturer would make the biscuits in batches.

Research

For the brief you have chosen:
- What are the reasons for adapting the products?
- Find out the needs and wants of the target group in your brief.
- Describe what changes would need to be made to the ingredients, preparation and/or cooking processes in the products you are designing, to make them suitable for the brief.
- Find out how the products could be produced in batches, and whether any special machinery would be required.
- Describe any changes that would need to be made to the presentation or packaging of the products.

Your specifications

Write down what your products will be like:
- Will they be suitable for vegetarians or people with special dietary needs?
- How will they be packaged, displayed or served?
- What portion size, colour, texture and flavour will they be?
- How will they be kept safe and fit to eat while they are being made, served or stored?
- How will the products all be kept the same during batch production?

Unit ⑥ Using ICT to support making

Food labelling

Food labels contain essential information for the consumer.

Most foods are sold in packaging, with a label giving **information** (in writing and/or pictures) about the product inside. Some of the information has to be shown by law. Some is shown voluntarily by the food producer to attract consumers to buy the product.

Food labels *should*:
▸ give consumers correct information so that they can choose between foods and understand what they are buying
▸ be honest by giving correct information about the product
▸ be clearly set out and easy to understand

Food labels *should not* mislead consumers about:
▸ what the food product is made from
▸ where the ingredients come from and how they were produced
▸ what size the product is
▸ how the product was made
▸ how long the product will be safe to eat

Food labelling is controlled by laws in different countries and by the European Union (EU). These laws apply to all food products that are made for sale to consumers and caterers. The laws do not apply to food that is eaten where it is bought (for example in a restaurant). However, all places where people buy food to eat (including small fast-food stalls) have to display a notice saying which foods they sell contain genetically modified (GM) ingredients.

Look at the food label below. The arrows point to the information that *must* be put on the label by law.

What else might you find on a food label?

1 ▸ The **name** of the food product.

2 ▸ The **amount** of the food product in the package shown as grams (g), millilitres (ml) or litres (l); or as a number of items, e.g. '5 apricot and nut cereal bars'.

▸ A letter 'e' means that the average weight of a pack must be accurate (agreed by the EU), but the weight of each pack may vary slightly.

3 ▸ A **date mark** to safeguard consumers against eating unfit food. There are different date marks for:

✦ **Perishable foods**, which are only safe to eat for a few days, and less than one month, have to show a 'sell by' or 'display until' date and must also give a 'use by' or 'eat by' date.

✦ Foods with a **shelf-life** (how long they are at their best) of up to 12 weeks have to show a 'best before day, month and year' date mark.

✦ Foods with a shelf-life of more than 12 weeks have to show a 'best before month and year' date mark.

✦ (Both of the above 'best before' date marks may have 'BBE' and then a date printed. This means 'best before the end' of the day, month, or year printed – so a bottle of lemonade, for example, that says 'BBE Jan 2002', unopened, will remain safe to use until January 31 2002.)

4 ▸ A list of **ingredients**, including any additives that have been used. These are listed in descending order of weight — i.e. the heaviest or greatest amount will be written first and the smallest, last. From February 2000, the amount of each ingredient also had to be included in this list. If water is added to a product and makes up more than 5% of the final weight, it must be included in the list. Some foods do not have to show a list of ingredients, e.g. fresh fruit and vegetables and single ingredient foods, e.g. sugar.

5 ▸ The **place of origin** (where the product was originally grown or produced).

6 ▸ Advice on **storing**, **preparing** and **cooking** the food product.

7 ▸ The **name** and **address** of the **food manufacturer**, **packager** or **importer**.

Here are some other things you often see on food labels:

▸ a **bar code** so that the product can be identified by computer. Companies use this technology to identify:

✦ the price, size, colour, flavour

✦ where and when the product was made (batch number)

✦ how much of it has been sold

✦ from which shop it was sold

▸ a **serving suggestion** (usually a picture to give the customer some ideas)

▸ **symbols** or **logos** to show whether the product is suitable for a particular diet or occasion, e.g. vegetarians, a barbecue, a low-fat diet.

Nutrition labelling

Many people try to look after their health by eating well and therefore like to know what is in the food they buy. Food manufacturers usually try to help people to eat healthily by giving information on the label about the nutrients in their products.

At present, nutrition labelling is voluntary in the EU, but if such information is given, it has to be written in a particular way. The only time that nutrition labelling *has* to be given is when the manufacturer makes a claim about a product, for example 'this product is low in fat and sugar' or 'suitable for babies under 6 months' or 'suitable for diabetics'.

There are computer programs available that work out the nutritional value of different foods and recipes. The results can be presented as graphs, tables or charts. Some programs also show the percentage of the recommended daily intake that each nutrient in the product provides.

The labels below show some different ways of presenting nutrition information. All nutrition labels *have* to show the amounts of nutrients in 100 g or 100 ml of the product, and may also show how much there is in a serving (for example one pot, one biscuit, 250 ml, etc.).

NUTRITIONAL INFORMATION
Typical values per 100g

Energy	1687kJ, 399kcal
Protein	Nil
Carbohydrate	87.1g
of which sugars	85.5g
Fat	5.8g
of which Saturates	1.3g
Fibre	Nil
Sodium	0.06g

NUTRITION INFORMATION

	AVERAGE VALUES	
	Per buscuit	Per 100g
ENERGY	237kJ, 56kcal	1991kJ 473kcal
PROTEIN	0.7g	5.6g
CARBOHYDRATE	9.0g	75.3g
of which sugars	3.8g	32.1g
FAT	2.0g	16.6g
of which Saturates	0.9g	7.4g
FIBRE	0.2g	1.7g
SODIUM	0.1g	0.5g

PER BISCUIT	56CALORIES	2.0g FAT

EU regulations stipulate how nutrition information should be listed on food labels.

QUESTIONS

1 Why is colour important on food labels?
2 Why are photographs or pictures of food products used on labels? Why must those photographs and pictures be accurate?
3 What colours do manufacturers often use for the following and why do you think they do so?
   a) special promotions, for example money off, 'three for two', '50% extra free'
   b) premium or top-quality products, for example coffee, chocolates, speciality biscuits
   c) products where children are the target group
4 How do some manufacturers get round the problem of printing lots of information on small packages, for example yogurt pots, snack foods, tubes of confectionery?
5 Why are the labels on the range of 'value' or 'low price' supermarket own brands of foods usually printed in only a few colours, without pictures or other decorations?
6 How is ICT used to design and produce food labels?
7 Choose three products with nutrition information on the labels and say which one is:
   ▶ Easiest to understand and why.
   ▶ The most difficult to understand and why. How do you think it could be improved?
8 Which groups of people would have difficulty in reading food labels, and how can manufacturers and food retailers help them?

NUTRITION INFORMATION

Typical values	Amount per 100g	Amount per serving (200g)
Energy	417kJ/99kcal	834kJ/198kcal
	56kcal	473kcal
Protein	6.4g	12.8g
Carbohydrate	10.4g	20.8g
(of which sugars)	(3.1g)	(6.3g)
Fat	3.6g	7.1g
(of which Saturates)	(0.2g)	(0.5g)
Fibre	2.9g	5.8g
Sodium	0.3g	0.7g

Per Serving (200g): 198 Calories 7.1g Fat

NUTRITION

	100g Dry Powder	1 Pint (57g) Marvel
Energy	1535kJ/361kcal	875kJ/206kcal
Protein	36.1g	20.6g
Carbohydrate	52.9g	30.2g
Fat	0.6g	0.3g
Vitamin A	72%RDA(575µg)	41%RDA(328µg)
Vitamin D	29%RDA(1.4µg)	17%RDA(0.83µg)
Calcium	160%RDA(1280mg)	91%RDA(730mg)

Unit 6 Food packaging

By the end of this section, you should be able to:

- Understand the reasons for packaging food.
- Identify the ways in which food is packaged.
- Identify the environmental problems caused by food packaging.
- Identify the ways in which ICT is used to design and manufacture packaging.

The two photographs below show food on sale in a modern supermarket, and a food shop as it might have looked before the first supermarkets appeared in the 1950s. In the modern supermarket, the food is displayed and sold in a variety of packaging materials, including different types of plastic. In the old shop, the main packaging materials are metal and cardboard; many other products would have been sold loose, and weighed and wrapped for each customer.

The growth of packaging technology – particularly the development of plastics – has enabled food manufacturers to increase the number of foods sold in packaged form. Packaging not only protects a product from damage, but also prolongs its shelf-life by slowing down or preventing natural decay and spoilage by micro-organisms.

Before plastics were developed, packaging was limited to materials such as metal, cardboard and glass.

The growth of technology has resulted in the development of many different kinds of packaging.

Types of food packaging	Reasons for use	Examples of food products
Aluminium cans (ring-pull lids)	Lightweight Product stays in good condition for a long time Convenient to use	Carbonated (fizzy) drinks
Tin plate steel cans	Food stays in good condition for a long time Difficult to tamper with a can, so food is secure	Fruits, vegetables, soups, cooked meat products, pies, puddings, sauces, baby foods, milk, cream

Types of food packaging	Reasons for use	Examples of food products
Plastic-coated (both sides) metal cans, aerosols and trays with easy-to-open ends, where the whole end or lid comes off (no opener required)	Convenient Easy to use Can be made to any shape or colour	Some baby foods and pet foods – more products being packaged in this way
Plastic bags, boxes, bottles, resealable packs, trays, cartons and pots	Lightweight Relatively cheap to produce Can be coloured and printed on Can be made into any shape Can be transparent Some are reusable by the consumer Can be moulded to the shape of the food product to keep air out Waterproof and greaseproof Some are flexible, so can be peeled off or torn to open Some can be used in a microwave oven, ordinary oven or freezer	Biscuits, cakes, meat products, bread, dairy foods and products, fruits and vegetables, sweets, snack foods, frozen foods, ready-made meals, drinks
Modified Atmosphere Packaging (MAP) (plastic)	Product is packed with a gas, e.g. nitrogen, to replace air, to make the product stay fresh for longer	Raw meat, ready-meals, fish
Controlled Atmosphere Packaging (CAP) (plastic)	Special plastic films are used to allow some gases in and keep some gases out, for foods that continue to respire ('breathe') after they have been picked	Fresh fruit and vegetables
Vacuum packaging (plastic)	The product is wrapped in strong plastic, and the air is sucked out and the plastic sealed, to keep out micro-organisms	Cooked meat products, cheeses, fish
Cardboard	Lightweight Relatively cheap to produce Can be coloured and printed	Cake and biscuit boxes, information sleeves for products sold in trays or pots, egg cartons, cereal boxes, separating layers for biscuits, cakes, snacks, display boxes and cards for sweets and snacks
Plastic-coated cardboard	Lightweight Keeps out air, light, smells, flavours Waterproof	Fruit juice, long-life milk, soups, sauces, wine
Glass	Transparent, fairly strong Easy to seal with metal or plastic lid Does not affect food in any way	Pickles, jams, pastes, vegetables, fruits, drinks, sauces

Cardboard, plastic and plastic-coated metal or cardboard are among the many materials used in modern food packaging.

The advantages of food packaging

Food packaging:

▶ keeps many foods fresh for longer because it prevents them from drying out, going 'soggy', being exposed to dirt, dust and flies, or going 'off'

▶ reduces the amount of food that is wasted, by keeping it in good condition for longer

▶ stops smells, colours, liquids, oils, or flavours transferring from one food to another when they are stored close together

▶ is convenient for consumers, who can quickly choose what they want from the supermarket shelves, transport the food home without spoiling it, and store and use the food easily

▶ is convenient for manufacturers and retailers who can print information on it, and transport and display foods easily

Using ICT

When a new food product is being planned, a team of designers will be given the job of designing suitable packaging. They will need to know several things about the product, for example:

▶ Its size, shape, colour.

▶ Is it liquid, solid, powder?

▶ Is it fragile?

▶ Will it go out of shape, break, melt easily or bruise if handled?

▶ How will the ingredients react with light, moisture, cold, heat, metals, plastics, paper, card?

▶ Will the product be refrigerated, frozen, or stored at room temperature?

▶ Its target group.

▶ Its composition.

A packaging designer puts the finishing touches on a design for a chocolate wrapper.

In mass production factories, packaging is usually controlled by computerized machines.

Computer-aided design (CAD) programs can be used to produce different simulated (pretend) designs to show what the packaging would look like with the product inside. CAD and computer-aided manufacture (CAM) can also be used to design and produce special moulds to make packaging from food-grade plastics or metal foil, for example for biscuits, cakes, ready-made meals, yogurt cartons.

Desk-top publishing (DTP) can be used to design and position the information that is to be printed on the package. It is important that when the package is formed on the production line, all the information is easy to see and in the right place and the right way round. Using DTP, the designers can try out different colours, fonts (styles of lettering), pictures, logos and patterns on the computer before they make a prototype package, which will save time and money.

When food products are mass-produced (large numbers are made at one time on a production line in a factory), computerized machines are often used to control the production line, and to package the products. Special sensors in the machines can detect how much of the product has been put into a package, and they send this information to the computer. The computer then sends a message back to the machine to tell it to stop filling the package, and to seal it. This all happens in a fraction of a second, and enables the manufacturer to control the whole process with only a few people.

Some products, e.g. decorated cakes for special occasions, are individually designed and hand-crafted. Cake decorators use a variety of tools to help them produce realistic designs, e.g. moulds, stencils, cutters, embossers (tools that leave a shape or pattern impressed into roll-out icing) and many others. Many of these tools are made using CAD and CAM.

The disadvantages of food packaging

Food packaging:

- can sometimes be difficult to open and use, especially by people who have weak hands and fingers
- produces much household waste, which has to be disposed of, and not all of which is biodegradable (it does not rot in the ground)
- uses up resources such as oil, trees and energy, which are needed to produce it
- is sometimes unnecessary, for example individually wrapped chocolate biscuits, which are wrapped in units of 6, then wrapped again to make a packet of 12
- increases the cost of the product
- increases the amount of litter that is dropped by people

Much concern has been expressed about packaging for food and other products, and there have been various schemes to encourage a reduction in the amount used, and the recycling (reusing) of packaging. The chart on the right shows how manufacturers, retailers and consumers can take more responsibility for the sensible use of food packaging:

About 90 % of the world's waste goes to landfill sites.

Newspapers and food packaging can cause pollution.

Manufacturers	Retailers	Consumers
Use the minimum amount of packaging by designing packaging that is thinner, but stronger, e.g. cans and plastic bottles.	Encourage manufacturers to use recycled materials and less packaging.	Recycle as much packaging and carrier bags as possible.
Use recycled materials where possible.	Encourage consumers to recycle by providing recycling centres in car parks or bins in shops.	Reuse packaging for other purposes, e.g. carrier bags as binbags, plastic boxes for storage.
Make it easy for packaging to be recycled by using easily removable labels and caps.	Use recycled cardboard and plastic cartons and wrappers used to transport products to the shops.	If possible, buy large packs or refills of some products, which use less packaging.
Encourage consumers to recycle packaging by printing logos on the label to say what the packaging is made from and whether it can be recycled.	Provide information about the importance of recycling.	Choose products that have packaging made from recycled materials.
		Look for logos on products that tell you if the packaging can be recycled.
		Ask shops and manufacturers not to use so much packaging.

QUESTIONS

1 Why is packaging used for foods?
2 Why are plastics used so much for food packaging?
3 What problems can food packaging cause?
4 Choose four different types of food product that you think use too much packaging. Say why this is, and how you think the packaging could be reduced without affecting the product inside.
5 Find out how packaging technology has improved the design of packaging and the safety of the following types of food product:
   a) liquids, for example milk
   b) individual yogurt desserts
   c) bottled baby foods
   d) cook-chill main meals

6 Using a computer, design your own package for one of the following food products:
   a) a can of vegetable soup
   b) a packet of pasta shapes
   c) a carton of breakfast cereal
   d) a ready-made dinner
Don't forget to include all the information that has to be included on the label by law. How will the packaging be put together?

At recycling centres, people can dispose of household waste including glass and plastic bottles, paper, cardboard and textiles.

RECYCLED PAPER

RECYCLE

PROJECT Food for teenagers

Fizzy drinks, hamburgers, pizzas and crisps are a convenient and popular source of quick energy for busy, active teenagers.

Several studies have shown that many teenagers:

▶ eat too much fat, sugar and salt (for example, in foods such as crisps, chips, sweets, chocolates, fizzy drinks, burgers, potato and corn snacks, pies, biscuits, sausages)
▶ don't eat enough fruit and vegetables
▶ don't get enough iron, calcium or folate
▶ don't do enough exercise

Other studies have shown that many teenagers:

▶ ignore healthy eating advice
▶ don't think about how healthy they might be in the future
▶ know the difference between 'junk' foods and healthy foods, but mostly choose to eat junk foods

By not eating healthily, teenagers may be storing up big problems for themselves when they become adults, for example:

Problem	Caused by	What does it do to you?
Being overweight or obese	Overeating Lack of exercise	Puts a strain on the heart, lungs, bones and joints Makes operations difficult and dangerous May increase risk of diabetes or cancer
Having tooth decay and gum disease	Eating too many sweet foods Not cleaning teeth properly or regularly	Makes the breath smell Spoils looks May lead to loss of teeth
Developing heart disease	Eating too much fat and salt Smoking Lack of exercise Stress (there are other reasons too)	Clogs up arteries that take blood to the heart May lead to chest pain when doing only a little exercise (angina) May lead to a heart attack and an early death
Osteoporosis (weak, fragile bones)	Not having enough calcium, phosphorus or vitamin D Not exercising enough when young to build up bone strength	Bones get weaker Bones break easily Spine develops a hump Back and joints very painful
Anaemia	Not having enough iron in the diet	Tiredness, weakness, poor concentration More likely to pick up infections
Not enough folate	Not eating enough fruit, vegetables, bread and cereals	May give birth to babies with spina bifida disability

Briefs

Choose one of the following:

1. Produce a poster or another medium (for example leaflet, key fob, sticker) to inform teenagers of why eating well is the right thing to do for their future health. Remember that research shows that people often ignore messages about healthy eating, so you need to present your information and message in a way that will attract teenagers. You can use desk-top publishing (DTP) and computer graphics to produce an eye-catching message.

2. Design and produce an alternative food to burgers and pizzas that could be sold in a fast-food restaurant and is targeted at teenagers. Try to include a good source of calcium and iron in the ingredients. Carry out some tasting sessions with teenagers and use ICT to present your results.

Research

❖ Conduct a survey among teenagers to find out:
  ▸ what they think and know about healthy eating
  ▸ what they think and know about the effects of what they eat on their future health
  ▸ what they feel about eating 'junk' foods
  ▸ where they like to eat and with which people
  ▸ how much exercise they take

❖ Find out how food manufacturers target teenagers for their food products.

❖ Find out how food manufacturers try to make their products appear more healthy.

❖ Find out why many fast-food restaurants target young children with gifts and special offers.

❖ Conduct a survey among adults to find out whether food choices change after being a teenager, and if so, how.

Your specification

If you choose the second brief, consider the following:

▸ Will any of your products be vegetarian?
▸ How will your products be prepared and cooked?
▸ How will your products be packaged?
▸ What flavours, textures and colours will your products contain?
▸ How will your products be labelled?
▸ What portion sizes will your products be?
▸ How will your products be kept safe to eat during preparation, cooking, packaging, transport, display and storage?

PROJECT Advertising food to children

A recent survey showed that children in the UK see more food and drink advertisements during children's television hours than children in any other European country. Almost all of the advertisements were for foods high in sugar, fat or salt, for example, sweets, breakfast cereals, and fizzy or fruit-flavoured sweet drinks.

Young children are less able to understand the reason for advertising — to persuade people to buy products — and so may believe everything that an advertisement says without asking whether what it says is really true. Research has found that television advertising is the most important influence on what children choose to eat. Many people are concerned that food advertising encourages children to have bad eating habits and a poor understanding of what to eat in order to be healthy.

Advertisements aimed at children are usually bright and eye-catching, and often feature cartoon characters.

Brief

Choose one of the following:

1. Design an advertisement (use DTP and computer graphics) to encourage young children to eat fruit and vegetables.
2. Design a healthy salad product that could be used for packed lunches, and prepare an advertisement to promote it to teenagers.
3. Design an eye-catching advertisement, possibly including an easy-to-remember rhyme or 'jingle', to promote one of the following products to children of junior school age:
   - fruit juice
   - pasta
   - vegetable soup
   - muesli
   - vegetable stir-fry ready-meal

Research

- Carry out a survey on food advertisements during children's and early evening television programmes, and list the groups of foods that are shown. If possible, carry this out over a week with other people (i.e. watch one day each) and pool your results.
- Find out how food manufacturers, restaurants and shops encourage children to notice and remember their products.
- Find out how people are encouraged to buy a food product again and again.
- Find out whether any countries in Europe do not allow advertisements to be shown to children.
- Suggest ways in which parents and carers can encourage children to be critical about food advertisements.
- Find out how ICT is used to produce food advertisements targeted at children, and why ICT is being used more and more for this purpose.

Unit (7) Producing batches

Production systems

Food products are made in both **large-** and **small-scale** production systems. Large-scale systems operate in factories that **mass-produce** large quantities of the same food product at a time, for example sliced bread, biscuits, sweets, pies, cakes, ice lollies and canned fruits. The production is usually controlled by computers, which are operated by a few workers. The computers control all the production processes, for example, weighing, cutting, time and speed of mixing, cooking, cooling and packaging.

Small-scale systems operate from smaller industrial units, shops or private homes, either producing **batches** of the same product, or specially designed single products, for example celebration cakes. **Batch production** is usually carried out by people, using their hands and some manufacturing aids such as mixing and cutting tools and machinery, measuring equipment (for example, electronic scales, temperature probes, measuring spoons), specially shaped moulds and ready-made packaging.

Large quantities of food are mass produced and packaged in factories.

Designing food products for batch production

When designing food products for batch production, these guidelines should be followed:

▶ The specification for each product should be easy to follow, with the criteria (standards) clearly set out, for example: how much of each ingredient it should contain, for how long it should be mixed, the minimum size the final product should be, and so on.
▶ Health and safety regulations must be carefully followed.
▶ Test batches of the product should be made to see how well it performs when made and packaged in batches, for example: do all items

Smaller quantities of food are prepared in catering kitchens.

in the batch cook evenly; do they all come out the same size; and do they stay in one piece when packaged?

▶ Products should be trialled and feedback from customers should be collected to find out whether it is necessary to make any modifications to the product.

Making food products in batches

To make sure that the individual food products in each batch are as similar to each other and of as good a quality as possible, these guidelines should be followed:

▶ Ingredients should be weighed accurately.

▶ The method of manufacture should be exactly the same each time, for example: length of time and speed of mixing, amount of mixture used for each product, cooking temperature and time. Equipment should be regularly checked to see that it is working accurately.

▶ Workers should be well trained and skilled at handling food.

▶ Finished products should be regularly checked for quality and accuracy of manufacture, for example: are they all the same size, weight, colour and flavour?

▶ Strict food hygiene rules should be followed to make sure that the finished products are safe to eat.

▶ For each product, a hazard analysis (see p36) should be carried out to identify and control health and safety risks that might arise during production.

A worker in a bakery checks a batch of biscuits for quality.

The cost of batch-produced products

A food manufacturer has to work out the cost of producing an item before deciding how much to sell it for. The individual items that have to be included in the calculation of the cost are called **overheads**. Overheads include:

- costs of ingredients and packaging
- costs of storing ingredients
- heating, lighting and delivery fuel costs
- workers' wages
- costs of running the building, for example: rent, business rates, removal of rubbish, supply of water
- costs of maintaining and replacing equipment
- cost of cleaning equipment and materials
- cost of faulty or damaged products that can't be sold

Buying and storing ingredients are two of the overheads that any business would have to pay for before it could start making a profit.

Other overheads might include fuel for delivery, and staff wages.

QUESTIONS

1 Why is it important that batch-produced food products are always made in exactly the same way?
2 What possible health and safety risks should a manufacturer of pies containing meat and dairy products be aware of?

PROJECT Batch production

Brief

A newly opened garden centre has asked a local catering business to provide it with a selection of six different batches of 'home-made' small cakes and cookies on a regular basis, for its coffee shop. The garden centre expects to make a 20 per cent profit on each cake or cookie it sells.

Design six specifications for the garden centre. Make a batch of *one* of the specifications you have designed, explaining how you will ensure that each item in that one batch is the same as all the others, and will be safe to eat.

Research

❖ Who will be the target group for these products?
❖ How will the products be presented and served at the coffee shop?
❖ What is the shelf-life (how long they 'keep') of small cakes and cookies?
❖ What manufacturing aids can be used to batch-produce the products?
❖ How will the products be mixed and baked?
❖ How will the manufacturer collect feedback about the products?
❖ How much will each product cost to make and sell to the garden centre?

Your specifications

▶ How will your products be prepared and cooked?
▶ How will your products be packaged?
▶ What flavours, textures and colours will your products contain?
▶ How will your products be labelled?
▶ What portion sizes will your products be?
▶ How will your products be kept safe to eat during preparation, cooking, packaging, transport, display and storage?

Unit ⑧ The world of professional designers

Developing new products

By the end of this section, you should be able to:

▶ Understand how designers work.
▶ Understand and identify how culture and lifestyle influence the design of products.
▶ Identify how products change over time.

New food products are constantly being designed and developed. In the past, most products were hand-crafted, and the amount made was limited by the time, energy and resources that an individual craft worker had available. Today, most products are made in factories using mass-production processes, and designers have more materials, ingredients, technologies, scientific knowledge and information available to help them design suitable products.

The driving force behind the design and development of new products comes from:

▶ What consumers **need** and **want** (for example, when greater numbers of women started going out to work and having less time to cook, ready-meals became increasingly popular).
▶ The development of **new technologies** as knowledge and awareness increases and changes.

When new products are being developed, the designer must take into account a number of issues, for example:

▶ There may be a wide range of possibilities they can consider, for example, what flavours to use for soups, and it may take some careful market research to decide which ones should be developed.
▶ Human capabilities and limitations, for example: how much strength is required to open a package, or how much of a carbonated (fizzy) drink the average person is able to drink from a can.
▶ The resources that are available, for example: money, materials, energy supply, ingredients, workers.
▶ People's needs and wants, which may change over time, and may vary in different areas of the country or world.
▶ If the product is to be exported to other countries, the designer must make sure that it is acceptable and will not cause offence, for example: because of an ingredient it contains, the design of the packaging or the name it has been given (which may be quite acceptable in one language, but spell an offensive or unsuitable word in another!).

Roles of professional designers

There are many different types of career in design. For the food industry, these include:

food product designer — designing new recipes and specifications for individual products and groups of products

industrial designer — designing machinery and food-processing systems for food manufacture

graphic designer — designing packaging and advertising material for food products

food technologist — designing new ways of manufacturing products, for example cook-chill for ready meals; ingredients, for example artificial flavourings; processing techniques, for example bubble technology to make products like ice-cream have a lighter texture, or blending oils and fats to make new types of spreads

retail designer — designing the internal layouts of, for example, supermarkets and restaurants, including planning the colour schemes and decorations used, and the most efficient way of serving customers

Packaging and advertising material are designed by graphic designers.

Retail designers plan the layout of shops and restaurants.

Travel has greatly increased our taste for foods from other countries.

'Fast foods' have become increasingly popular in the UK, although many people are concerned about their nutritional value.

Lifestyle, culture and product design

Designers have to be aware of changing trends in lifestyle and the influence of these, and of different cultures, on what people choose to eat. People travel abroad more frequently than they did in the past, which has led to an increase in the number of food products and places to eat that are based on different cultures and lifestyles.

Some cultures have distinctive ways of preparing and cooking foods, for example, many Mexican foods have a hot chilli flavour, while American foods tend to be sweet, and Indian foods spicy. Foods can be used to express the relationships between people; for example, in some cultures, the most powerful individuals have the first and best choice of foods. Foods are also used to celebrate important occasions, for example holy days, weddings and ceremonies such as Bar Mitzvahs.

Lifestyles and cultural habits tend to change over time. Modern Western cultures have in recent years emphasised the harm that food can do to health; for example, by eating too much fat and sugar, people can develop heart disease and cancer. This has led to the design of products with lower fat and sugar contents, to cater for people who are concerned about their food intake.

At the same time, food culture has been greatly influenced by the American fast-food style of eating. These products often have a high fat and sugar content. Designers have also developed products to cater for this style of eating, and for the increasing trend for eating snack foods instead of large meals.

QUESTIONS

1 How do manufacturers find out what new products consumers might need or want?

2 List five food products that cater for people who want less fat or sugar in their diet.

3 List five food products that come from other countries but are eaten regularly in this country. Say which countries they come from.

PROJECT Authentic ready-made meals

Brief

A supermarket chain has carried out research that shows that many of its customers find ready-made meals to be inauthentic (not like the real foods from other countries). The company has decided to launch a new range of authentic meals from different countries, using traditional ingredients, preparation and processing methods. Design a range of ready-made meals that could be served in the chilling cabinet of the supermarket.

Research

❖ Which meals from other countries are the most popular?
❖ Which special ingredients can be obtained in this country?
❖ How will the special ingredients be imported (fresh, dried, frozen, canned, etc.)?
❖ What preparation and processing methods will be used?
❖ What special equipment will be needed?
❖ How will the products be packaged?
❖ How will the products be marketed and promoted?

Your specification

Write down what the products will be like:
▶ Will they be vegetarian or non-vegetarian?
▶ Will they be served hot or cold?
▶ How will they be kept safe during manufacture, transport and storage?
▶ How will they be priced?
▶ What serving suggestions (what to serve with the meal) will be given on the packaging?

Unit (9) Selecting ingredients

By the end of this section, you should be able to:
▸ Understand the difference between a survey and a questionnaire.
▸ Understand the value of surveys and questionnaires in market research.
▸ Identify suitable questions to ask and information to find out.

Carrying out surveys and questionnaires

Surveys and questionnaires are frequently used in market research to find out:
▸ what people think about something
▸ what people know about something
▸ what people like and dislike
▸ what is available for people to use or buy

Surveys

A survey is used to take a general look at something, and usually involves counting or measuring, for example:
▸ the number of food shops in an area
▸ the number of different types of fruit for sale
▸ the amount of fat in different types of cheese
▸ the most popular flavour or packaging for a food product
▸ how often people go food shopping
▸ what transport people use to go shopping
▸ the size and location of food shops in an area
▸ what percentage of people in a group are vegetarian
▸ how much of a food product is sold in a given time (usually recorded by computer in a supermarket)

Questionnaires

A questionnaire is used to find out information about a particular topic, by asking people specific questions, for example:
▸ what they think about the amount of packaging used in a food product
▸ what they think about fast-food restaurants
▸ what type of cooker they would prefer to own
▸ what they think about buying food using the Internet
▸ whether they would want an out-of-town supermarket to open in their area
▸ which sample of a food product they prefer and why

A market researcher counts the number of cars entering a supermarket parking lot, in order to find out what means of transport people use to go shopping.

Questionnaires are a useful source of information for market researchers.

agree very much

agree

don't mind

disagree

disagree very much

Why are surveys and questionnaires useful to food manufacturers and retailers?

Surveys are useful because they provide information about:
▶ how well a food product is selling
▶ what types of food product sell well in certain areas or types of shop
▶ what products are bought by certain groups of people
▶ what type of packaging, flavouring, size, colour, etc., is most popular for a food product
▶ what other food manufacturers and retailers (competitors) are producing and selling

Questionnaires are useful because they provide information about:
▶ why people buy certain products
▶ why they shop for food at certain times and places
▶ what their needs and wants for food products are
▶ whether a food product or shop meets their needs and wants
▶ what type of food product they would like to be able to buy

Watch points!

▶ Before you start drawing up your questionnaire, be clear about what you want to know and why you want to know it. This will help you to draw conclusions from your results.
▶ People are not always truthful when filling in questionnaires, so you may need to back up your results with other information. For example, most school children may say that they like to eat healthily, but every lunch-time they choose chips, doughnuts and a fizzy drink instead of salad, fruit and water!
▶ People will get bored if they have to write long answers in a questionnaire, so only ask for a short answer, for example: *yes/no/don't know*

or use scales such as the one on the left or the one below:
1 (least liked)............10 (most liked)

or ask people to tick a box from a multiple-choice answer, for example:
do you think this soup is:
❏ *too spicy?*   ❏ *just right?*   ❏ *bland (not enough spice)?*

▶ The more people you ask, the more realistic your results and conclusions will be.

ⓆUESTIONS

1 A large supermarket chain is considering opening a new branch in a certain area. What information do they need to find out in order to decide whether this is a good idea?
2 How might they go about getting this information?

Unit 9

Sampling food products

By the end of this section, you should be able to:

▶ Understand what sensory analysis means.
▶ Identify different ways of sampling foods.
▶ Identify different ways of presenting food sampling results.

Sensory analysis

'Analysis' means to look at and study something closely, in order to understand:

▶ what it is made of
▶ how it works
▶ how it affects other things
▶ how it could be changed or improved

In **sensory analysis**, the senses of sight, touch, smell, taste and hearing are used for this purpose.

When food products are analysed, the **analyst** (the person doing the analysis) will use sensory analysis to study:

▶ the appearance, texture (feel), aroma (smell), flavour and sound of a product
▶ the effect that altering something in the product (for example the amount or type of flavouring) has on what people think about it
▶ how one food product compares with another similar product, for example, for flavour, appearance, image and quality

Food manufacturers employ trained testers to:

▶ Try samples of food products.
▶ Write down their opinions of those food products by using words to describe something about them, for example, the texture of a bread roll could be described as: *chewy*, *crusty*, *dry*, *floury*, *heavy*, or *spongy*; the flavour of an orange drink could be described as *acid*, *tangy*, *fruity*, *bitter* or *sour*.
▶ Rate the food products on a **scale**, for example: *most liked — least liked*; *saltiest — least salty*; *smoothest – least smooth*.
▶ Compare one food product with others for particular characteristics, for example moistness, oiliness, hardness, chewiness.
▶ Describe their likes and dislikes about a product, for example, *lovely*, *revolting*. These types of word are called **hedonic descriptors**.
▶ Describe what they feel and believe about a product, for example, that it is *healthy*, *natural*, *traditional*, or *artificial*. These types of word are called **attitudinal descriptors**.

A food tester tastes a cake sample and records her findings.

You can carry out food sampling tests quite easily, to find out what people think of your food products. Here are some tips to follow when carrying out any food sampling tests:

Samples of different kinds of muffins, prepared for tasting.

▶ The more people you ask to take part in your test, the more useful your results will be. The descriptions of tests on the next page tell you the minimum (smallest) number of people you should ask.

▶ Always give each food sample a **code number**, which only you should know. In this way, the opinion or description your testers give will not be influenced by knowing what they are tasting.

▶ Don't give out the samples in a particular order — muddle them up, so that the testers do not try all the samples in the same order as each other.

▶ Always include a **control sample** (one that has not had anything altered).

▶ Give the testers a glass of water to drink between tasting each sample, to clear their taste buds and mouth before they try the next one.

Carrying out sensory analysis tests

First, decide what you want to test. Examples of tests that can be done include:

▶ What effect does changing the amount of salt/sugar/herbs/spices in the product have on its overall flavour and acceptability?

▶ Can people tell the difference between two identical products if something in one of the products, for example the colour, is changed slightly?

▶ What do people think about a home-made tomato soup compared with a canned or dried tomato soup?

▶ What do people think about the suitability of one type of product for a vegetarian compared with another type?

QUESTIONS

1 Why is it important to have a drink of water before tasting each sample of food?

2 Why is it important that each sample of food tested be prepared and cooked in exactly the same way?

3 Why do food manufacturers use sensory analysis tests?

Food sampling tests

Test name and reason for doing it	Minimum number of people to ask	What to do	What to conclude from the results
Paired comparison test If you predict that altering something in a food product will have an effect on it, this test should tell you whether or not your predictions were right.	6	▸ give each person several pairs of food samples ▸ in each pair, one sample should be the control and the other should be different, according to what you are testing e.g. less fat, more spices; ask them a question, e.g. which one is spicier, or which one is crisper?	▸ add up the right answers ▸ if 6 out of 6 people choose the sample that has been altered, each time, then it means that alteration has made a noticeable difference to the product
Triangle test Shows up small differences between similar products.	5	▸ give each person sets of three samples, two of which are identical, the other one being the odd one out ▸ ask them to identify the odd one out in each set of three	▸ add up the number of right answers ▸ if four out of five people get the right answer it means that whatever was changed in the odd one out was different enough to be noticed
Ranking test Shows up noticeable differences and similarities between samples.	10	▸ give each person a set of samples to try ▸ ask them to rank them in order according to what you are testing, e.g. greasiness, redness, sweetness, sourness	▸ for each person, write down the order they put the samples into ▸ add up the score for each sample, and see which samples are different from and similar to each other (see chart)
Rating test Shows which product is preferred the most or least, or is judged to have the most or least of a particular characteristic.	20	▸ give each person a set of samples to try ▸ ask them to rate the samples according to what you are testing, e.g. preference (most liked – least liked) or flavour (most fruity – least fruity)	▸ add up the ratings for each sample ▸ plot the results on a pie chart, bar chart or frequency distribution graph (see examples)

Ranking test for mixed vegetable soup

Most salty to least salty

Samples:

Code number given to tester	Actual sample not known by tester
5189	A (1st [most salt added])
8731	B (2nd)
6425	C (3rd)
9659	D (4th [least salt added])

Results:

Tester	Order of samples				Rank sum
	A	B	C	D	
Sam	1	3	2	4	10
Ahmed	1	2	3	4	10
Jo	2	1	3	4	10
Jane	1	2	4	3	10
Andrew	2	1	3	4	10
Leon	1	2	4	3	10
Fran	1	4	3	2	10
Kyle	1	4	2	3	10
Jade	1	3	2	4	10
Josh	1	3	2	4	10
TOTAL	12	25	28	35	100

The results show that the testers could tell that samples B and C are similar, but that sample A is a lot different to sample D.

Rating Test

Results of rating test for most and least liked vegetable curry. Number of testers: 20

Sample curry — Number of testers who:

	liked most	liked a little	neither liked nor disliked	disliked a little	disliked most
A	1	3	5	6	5
B	12	4	2	1	1
C	3	4	9	2	2
D	7	5	3	3	2

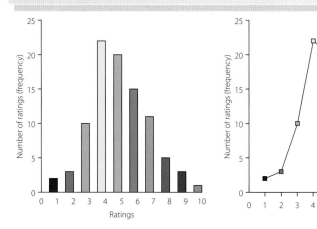

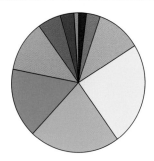

Ratings can be represented in a variety of ways.

PROJECT Special diets

The food that a person eats every day makes up their **diet**. For most people, eating a mixture of foods every day, like those in the pictures below, is the best way to stay healthy and fit.

In order to remain fit and healthy, it is essential to follow a balanced diet and eat a variety of foods.

Some people have to follow a special diet because:
▸ they may need to lose weight
▸ they may have an illness, for example, heart disease, anaemia or diabetes, that is affected, or needs to be controlled, by what they eat
▸ certain foods make them ill, so they have to avoid eating them, for example coeliac disease and nut allergy sufferers

For some people, it is hard to change from their usual eating habits to a special diet, so they have to be encouraged and helped by their doctor, dietician and family.
    Food manufacturers and retailers also offer help by:
▸ producing information leaflets and meal-planning ideas
▸ adapting certain food products to meet special needs, for example by reducing fat, sugar and salt, or by increasing fibre or calcium
▸ labelling food products to show which are suitable or unsuitable for special diets, for example 'gluten free' for coeliacs, 'nut free' or 'may contain traces of nuts' for nut allergy sufferers
▸ labelling food products to show which nutrients they contain and their energy values

Brief

For one of the special diets and target groups below, design a main meal (main course and pudding) that could be sold as cook-chill or frozen products:

▶ a low-fat diet for someone with heart disease
▶ a low-sugar diet for someone with diabetes

Gluten-free cereal products are available for people who suffer from coeliac disease.

▶ a low-salt diet for someone with high blood pressure
▶ a high-fibre diet for someone with chronic constipation
▶ a low-energy diet for someone trying to reduce their weight
▶ a nut-free diet for someone with a severe allergy

Research

❖ Find out how and why a special diet will help the target group you have chosen.
❖ Identify which foods would be suitable/unsuitable for this special diet and explain the reasons for this.
❖ Find out how food manufacturers and retailers try to help your chosen target group and give examples to illustrate this.
❖ Identify any problems that might occur during the preparation and manufacture of the food products for your target group.
❖ Find out about any organizations that offer help to people in your chosen target group.

Your specification

Write down what your products will be like:

▶ What portion size will each be?
▶ Will they be vegetarian or non-vegetarian?
▶ Why and how will the products be suitable for the target group?
▶ Will they be served hot or cold?
▶ How will they be packaged and labelled?
▶ What advice might you include on the labelling?
▶ How will they be kept safe during preparation, cooking, transport and storage?
▶ How much will each product cost to make and buy?

PROJECT Food production in a hospital

Food production in a hospital is a type of **welfare catering**. Welfare caterers have to produce food on a limited budget and do this in a way that is cost-effective and not wasteful. School meals and food for people in residential care are other types of welfare catering.

People go into hospital for a number of reasons, for example:

▶ to be treated for and recover from an accident, in which they may have lost blood, broken bones, received head injuries or suffered burns and scalds

▶ to have an operation, which could be minor (for example, having ingrowing toenails removed), or major (for example, open-heart surgery)

▶ to receive treatment for an illness, for example, a chest infection, cancer, heart disease, food poisoning

▶ to have a baby

▶ to receive treatment and care for a condition, for example, diabetes, physical disability, arthritis, infirmity through old age

Eating good-quality food in hospital is just as important as good nursing and medical care. In the UK, the National Health Service (NHS) and private hospitals provide millions of meals every year. In some other countries, friends and relatives have to bring food into hospital to feed patients themselves.

Usually, patients are given a choice of food from a menu like the one shown in the picture. These are given out the day before to give the caterers enough time to prepare the meals that people have chosen. When the menu is planned, the following points must be taken into account:

▶ it must cater for different types of diet, for example, full (normal), light, liquid only, or special (for example, low fat or salt, diabetic)

▶ it must cater for people with different needs, for example, vegetarians, or people with food allergies or certain religious beliefs

▶ it must be easy to understand and fill out

▶ it must clearly show which items are suitable for diabetics, vegetarians, etc.

The quality of hospital food needs to be high for several reasons, including the following:

▶ Patients who are ill and weak are more likely to suffer from food poisoning if the standard of food safety in the hospital kitchen is poor.

Hayfield Hospital

LUNCH

Name _____
Ward _____

Diet Label
Key to Diet Codes
R = Reducing

SUPPER

Name _____
Ward _____

Diet Label
Key to Diet Codes
R = Reducing
F = Modified Fat
D = Diabetic (Portion Sizes)
✳ = Modified Recipe
V = Vegetarian

All our portions are Standard
For alternatives mark   Small, ☐   or Large ☐
PLEASE MARK ONE ITEM FROM EACH SECTION

		Diet Code				Ptns
1	COTTAGE PIE WITH GRAVY	R	F	D		2
2	JACKET POTATO & BAKED BEANS	R	F	D	V	2
3	WHLML GRATED CHEDDAR CHEESE S'WICH		R	D	V	2
4	PARSLEY POTATOES	R	F	D	V	2
5	MIXED VEGETABLES	R	F	D	V	
	HOMEMADE BAKEWELL TART					
	RICH CHOCOLATE WHIP					
	SEASONAL FRUIT	R	F	D	V	
	STRAWBERRY BLANCMANGE	R		D*	V	
	BROWN BREAD	R	F	D	V	1
	WHITE BREAD	R	F	D	V	1
	LOW FAT SPREAD	R	F	D	V	
	BUTTER					
		R	F	D	V	
		R	F	D	V	
	DIET CHOICE	**R**	**F**	**D**	**V**	

*, and Asian Vegetarian meals are available

Hayfield Hospital

BREAKFAST

Name _____
Ward _____

Diet Label
Key to Diet Codes
R = Reducing
F = Modified Fat
D = Diabetic (Portion Sizes)
✳ = Modified Recipe
V = Vegetarian

How to complete your Menu:-
Please use blue or black pen
NOT RED
Mark your choice by making a cross in the box

☒

Special Diet
Are you on a Special Diet?
There are the Codes to help you choose:-

R = Reducing
F = Modified Fat
D = Diabetic (Portion Sizes)
✳ = Modified Recipe
V = Vegetarian

Please Mark Your Diet at the bottom of the Menu.

Should you wish to see a member of the Catering Staff, please mark the box below.

ENJOY YOUR MEAL

PLEASE MARK ONE OF THE FOLLOWING

		Diet Code				Ptns
		R	F	D	V	1
1	ORANGE JUICE					

PLEASE MARK ONE OF THE FOLLOWING

		R	F	D	V	1
2	PORRIDGE	R	F	D	V	1
3	HIGH PROTEIN PORRIDGE (only on Dietician's advice)					
4	WEETABIX – 1 PORTION	R	F	D	V	1
5	WEETABIX – 2 PORTIONS	R	F	D	V	2
6	BRAN FLAKES	R	F	D	V	1
7	CORNFLAKES	R	F	D	V	1

PLEASE MARK UP TO TWO OF THE FOLLOWING

8	BROWN BREAD	R	F	D	V	1
9	WHITE BREAD	R	F	D	V	1
10	WHOLEMEAL ROLL	R	F	D	V	2
11	WHITE ROLL	R	F	D	V	2

PLEASE MARK ONE OF THE FOLLOWING

12	LOW FAT SPREAD			D	V	
13	BUTTER				V	

PLEASE MARK ONE IF REQUIRED

14	MARMALADE	F			V	
15	JAM	F			V	

☐ REDUCING DIET CHOICES
☐ MODIFIED DIET CHOICES
☐ DIABETIC DIET CHOICES
N.B. Please note that sliced bread and additional spreads will be provided from the Ward Kitchen

Hospital dieticians play an important role in the care of patients.

Hospital menus must cater for different needs.

▶ If the food is well cooked, its flavour, colour, texture and nutrients will be preserved, giving patients the most benefit.
▶ If the food is well presented, it will tempt patients with a poor appetite to eat it.

A number of people are involved in food production in a hospital. Many hospitals have **dieticians**, who work with:
▶ The **caterers**, to prepare menus for special diets.
▶ The **medical staff**, to decide on the best treatment for a patient.
▶ The **patients**, to advise them about feeding themselves when they go home from hospital.

Catering managers are in charge of:
▶ Planning menus.
▶ Ordering food supplies.
▶ Supervising the preparation, cooking and serving of meals.
▶ Training staff.
▶ Health and safety.
▶ Providing food for patients, visitors (in restaurants) and staff who work in the hospital (in canteens).

PROJECT

One catering manager may be in charge of more than one hospital in an area, and have assistants to help in each hospital.

Kitchen superintendents are in charge of running one or more kitchens in a hospital. They have to make sure that meals are prepared correctly and on time and delivered to the right wards. **Cooks**, usually led by a head cook, do specific jobs in each kitchen. **Porters** are responsible for delivering meals to the wards.

Sometimes food is prepared in small kitchens attached to wards. Usually, light meals, snacks or special diet foods are prepared by nurses in these kitchens, and there may also be a small kitchen on children's wards for parents to use.

A number of problems associated with producing food for patients in a hospital may have to be overcome. These include:

▶ In many hospitals, especially old ones with lots of separate buildings, the kitchens may be a long way from the wards. This may make it difficult to keep the food hot (special heated trolleys are used for this) and appetizing, and on time to serve it.

▶ Meal times have to fit in with the (usually) strict routine of the hospital, and the food may have to be kept hot and fresh while, for example, a doctor finishes checking all the patients in a ward.

▶ The amount of money available to spend on producing food will be strictly controlled and may limit what can be provided.

Food is usually delivered to patients on heated trolleys.

Briefs

Choose one of the following:

1. Design a menu for two days (three meals a day) for patients in a ward that deals with broken bones and bone operations. Some patients are unable to sit up to eat.

2. Design a menu for two days (three meals a day) for a children's ward, which includes babies and children up to 14 years old.

3. Design a menu for two days (three meals a day) for patients on a ward that deals with diabetic patients.

4. Design a menu for two days (three meals a day) for patients on a ward that deals with heart disease.

5. Design a menu for two days (three meals a day) for one of these patients with special needs:

   someone who is anaemic (needs more iron)

   someone who is a coeliac (cannot eat gluten – the protein found in wheat and some other cereals)

   someone who is a Hindu and has a broken hip bone

   someone who is a vegetarian and has lost a lot of blood in an accident

Carry out your research and produce a specification.

Produce one complete main midday meal for the brief you have chosen.

Research

❖ Identify the particular needs of the patients you are considering, for example:
   ▶ which nutrients they particularly need and why
   ▶ which foods they can and cannot eat and why
   ▶ which foods they should avoid eating and why
   ▶ how easy or difficult it is for them to feed themselves

❖ Find out how meals are usually served in modern hospitals, for example, what types of plates, bowls and cutlery are used; how each meal is identified for particular patients; how drinks are served.

❖ Find out how much money is usually spent on each meal.

❖ Identify ways of making the food appetizing.

❖ Identify how the colour, texture, flavour and nutrients will be preserved during the preparation, cooking and serving of the meal.

❖ Identify how the meal will be kept safe to eat during preparation, cooking and serving.

Unit 10 Designing for markets

Production systems

By the end of this section, you should be able to:

- Understand that different food products are designed to be made in large or small quantities.
- Understand the difference between 'one-off' and 'high-volume' production.
- Identify the different processes used by manufacturers to make food products.
- Understand how safety and quality are built in to the design process.

Food products (like other products) are made in a **production system**. Production systems have three parts:

Input What goes in, for example, ingredients, packaging and energy.

Process What goes on, i.e. how the product is made.

Output What comes out, i.e. the finished product and any waste or unused materials.

Many food products are made all year round, in very large numbers, so that consumers can buy them often. This is called '**mass**' or '**high-volume**' production.

Some food products are made only at certain times of the year, in smaller numbers, for example at Christmas time, or are designed and made for individual customers, for example celebration cakes. This is called '**one-off**' production.

High-volume production has to be carefully researched and designed so that:

- each finished product is the same as all the others (this is called **repetitive quality**)
- each product is produced in a safe and clean way
- all the ingredients needed are available throughout the year

'One-off' celebration cakes are usually decorated by hand.

One-off production has to be carefully researched and designed so that:

▶ it meets the specific needs and requirements of the customer, so that expensive mistakes are avoided

▶ just enough products are made, so that not too many are left over and have to be sold at a loss

As more of a product is made, and fewer people are involved in the manufacture, the less it costs to produce each individual item. Customers generally expect to pay less for high-volume products than one-off products, which require more time and people to produce.

Designing a product

Once a manufacturer has carried out market research and decided that a new product is needed, the final design can be started. Manufacturers often use computer-aided design (CAD) to make this process simpler and more efficient.

The design must include *how* the product will be made, i.e:

▶ what machinery will be required
▶ how the mixture will be made
▶ how it will be cut/shaped/rolled out/mixed, etc.
▶ how it will be cooked/chilled/preserved
▶ how it will be packaged and stored
▶ how it will be distributed
▶ how the product will be kept safe while it is being made

Using a CAD system, a designer can work out a packaging design in three dimensions.

CAD can be used to work out some of these factors, for example, the design of a cutting or shaping machine, the way products pass through an oven to be cooked, or the way the packaging is put on.

Manufacturing processes

Manufacturers often use computer-aided manufacture (CAM) to make high-volume products. CAM uses special electronic **sensors**, which collect information about each product (for example, weight, temperature, colour, texture) as it is being made. This information is sent back to a computer, which then sends instructions back to the production line, for example, to cool the product, add more product, or cook for longer. Information that is sent and used in this way is called **feedback**.

Manufacturers use various processes to make food products. Some processes are carried out by machines (often controlled by computer), and some are carried out by people.

Process	Examples	Machine or people
Separating	Draining water from washed vegetables. Sieving flour from milled wheat. Filtering impurities from oil.	machine machine machine
Heating	Cooking ingredients for ready meals. Heating milk to destroy harmful bacteria.	machine machine
Cooling	Chilling cooked food, e.g. chicken pie filling. Freezing vegetables or fresh meat.	machine machine
Mixing	Beating cake mixtures. Mixing dry ingredients e.g. for muesli. Blending sauces.	machine machine machine
Breaking up into smaller pieces	Chopping, shredding, slicing, mincing, dicing, grating.	machine or people
Shaping	Using a mould, e.g. for chocolates or ice lollies. Using a cutter, e.g. for biscuits. Using a shaped nozzle, e.g. for icing or pasta shapes.	machine or people
Coating	With chocolate, e.g. for biscuits. With batter, e.g. for fish or chicken pieces. With a glaze, e.g. egg on pastry or jelly on fruit.	machine or people
Decorating	With a variety of components, e.g. sugar strands, fruit, vegetables, chocolate, icing, cream.	machine or people
Packaging	By filling containers or wrapping and sealing products.	machine or people

Quality assurance and quality control

When people buy a food product, they need to feel confident that the product is safe and of a good quality. **Quality assurance** is a type of promise or guarantee that the manufacturer makes to the consumer that the product is:

▶ safe to eat

▶ made to a particular standard

- well designed
- honestly produced and described on the label
- suitable for the purpose it was designed for

Quality control is a method used by the manufacturer when they design a product, to make sure that the product does not fall below the standard required. As the product is designed, each stage is examined so that any problems that could arise can be corrected to avoid hazards or expensive and wasteful mistakes, and to check that the product meets the specification.

HACCP (Hazard Analysis of Critical Control Points) is the name given to an important type of quality control that is used in all parts of the food industry, for example, farms, restaurants, shops, factories and distribution companies. It aims to ensure that food products are made, stored and transported as safely and hygienically as possible.

The types of hazard that could occur when food products are made, stored or transported include:

- the growth of food-poisoning bacteria in the food, in the food preparation area or on equipment
- items falling into the food, for example from machinery
- packaging or storage faults allowing micro-organisms to enter and grow in the food
- invasion of the premises or equipment by pests, for example cockroaches or rats
- slippery floor surfaces in food premises, which put workers in danger
- pollution of water, air or the local environment by chemicals, rubbish or waste materials
- poor hygiene habits of people who handle the food

The environmental health department of the local council will want to make sure that food businesses have carried out a HACCP, and will regularly check that they are closely monitoring each stage of their business, in order to protect the consumer from unsafe food or practices.

Hazard Analysis of Critical Control Points (HACCP) aims to ensure that food products are made, stored and transported hygienically.

QUESTIONS

1 Why are one-off products usually more expensive than high-volume products? Give an example of each.
2 Why does CAD make designing new products a simpler and more efficient process?

Unit 10

Buying food

By the end of this section, you should be able to:

▶ Compare how food is bought by the consumer, the retailer, and the manufacturer.

▶ Identify points to think about when buying food.

Where do consumers buy their food?

Most food is bought in **supermarkets**. There are several different supermarket companies in the UK, but four well-known ones — Tesco, Asda, Safeway and Sainsbury's — sell most of the food in the country. Supermarkets sell thousands of different food products, and aim to offer consumers lots of choice. Out-of-town **superstores** have become very popular and offer lots of other goods and services besides food, including banking, petrol, dry-cleaning and garden goods. People also buy food from:

▶ open-air markets

▶ farm shops and farmers' markets

▶ small, independent supermarkets

▶ specialist shops, for example fishmongers and bakeries

▶ box schemes that deliver food, for example fruit and vegetables, to your door

▶ home delivery schemes operated by supermarkets via the Internet

Tesco is one of the four most popular supermarkets in the UK.

Specialist food shops are usually more expensive than supermarkets, but may offer the consumer a better variety of a particular product.

Where do retailers buy their food?

Large retail companies, for example supermarkets, often buy food direct from **farmers** and **producers**. They make a contract with the farmer or producer, who has to have the food ready at a certain time for the retailer to sell. Retailers ask for the food to be produced to a set standard, for example a particular size, colour, shape or ripeness. Farmers and producers often also package and label the food for the retailer.

Retailers also buy from food **manufacturers**. They buy either directly from the manufacturer or from a **wholesaler**. Wholesalers buy food from manufacturers and sell it on to retailers from large warehouses.

Retailers buy foods from all over the world so that their customers can have foods that are out of season, for example strawberries only grow in the UK in the summer, but can be bought from other countries for the rest of the year. Many foods travel thousands of kilometres before they arrive in the shops. Most food is sent to retailers in lorries, from central **distribution centres**.

Many kinds of fruit and vegetable are grown especially for sale to supermarkets.

Goods are stored in wholesalers' warehouses before being distributed to retailers.

How do retailers know how much food to buy?

Almost all food products have a bar code on their label. Each bar code represents a number, which is unique to the food product on which it is printed. The bar code number is programmed into a computer, and is 'read' by a laser scanner at the checkout.

For each food retailer, the computers in their supermarkets are linked to central computers at the Head Office. Every time a food product is sold in a supermarket, the information from the bar code is recorded. At the Head Office, the computers record how much of every food product each supermarket sells. This information goes out to distribution centres, which use it to keep each supermarket supplied with food products as it sells them.

Making sure that supermarkets are supplied with products as they need them is called 'stock control'. Computer technology has helped retailers to do this more easily and accurately. Sometimes the information goes directly to manufacturers, who supply the supermarkets directly from the factory, with stock including bakery products, milk and dairy products.

Bar codes are printed on every packaged product.

Bar codes are scanned and recorded in a central computer.

Bar codes also provide information for the customer.

Where do manufacturers buy their foods?

Large manufacturers often own farms, plantations and orchards and control what, when and how food is produced. They often buy **components** (individual ingredients) for food products from other manufacturers, for example flavourings, packaging, sugar, fats and cake icings. Like retailers, they may have contracts with the farmers and producers who supply them with foods. Some manufacturers produce, manufacture and sell food products directly from their farms, for example cheese, yogurt and ice cream.

Points to think about when buying food

How clean are the premises (the place where the food is sold)?
Check

▸ the floor, the shelves, the chiller cabinets and freezers
▸ is fresh food, e.g. cooked meats, fish, raw meat, etc. covered?
▸ are there animals around?
▸ are the assistants wearing clean overalls; do they have clean hands?

How fresh is the food on sale?
Check

▸ the 'use by' and 'best before' dates on the packaging
▸ are fruits and vegetables crisp and colourful or limp, wrinkled and dull?
▸ is fresh meat a good colour and moist, or is it dull and dry?

Do you know what is in the food?
Check

▸ the ingredients and nutrients lists on the label
▸ information labels and leaflets about the foods on sale, e.g. do they contain nuts?

Are you getting value for money?
Check

▸ the price per kg, 100 ml or portion, and compare it with other products
▸ are the portion sizes big enough?
▸ are you paying for a lot of packaging and fancy labels?
▸ could you make the same product yourself at a fraction of the price?

QUESTIONS

1 Why are supermarkets the most popular places to buy food?
2 Why is it often cheaper to buy food from open-air markets?
3 Why have a lot of small food shops, for example butchers, bakeries, and fishmongers, closed down in the past few years?
4 Why is it often cheaper to buy foods directly from the farmer?
5 What effects do out-of-town superstores have on:
   ▸ the environment
   ▸ poor and elderly people
   ▸ town centres?
6 How do supermarkets encourage people to buy food from them?
7 How do food manufacturers encourage people to buy their products?

Unit ⑩   Storing food

By the end of this section, you should be able to:

▶ Understand the difference between perishable and non-perishable foods.
▶ Identify the responsibilities of manufacturers, retailers, caterers and consumers in the safe storage of foods.

The length of time that a food can be stored before it starts to 'go off', and becomes unfit to eat, is called its **shelf-life**. Different foods have different shelf-lives, depending on how **perishable** they are (how quickly they 'go off').

Very perishable foods, for example raw meat and fish, cream, milk, poultry, cream cheese, meat pâtés and pies, and fresh strawberries, have a short shelf-life and must be stored by **chilling** or **freezing**, and used up quickly. Less perishable foods, for example fresh root and green vegetables, fresh fruit, bread and cakes, have slightly longer shelf-lives, and can be stored at **ambient temperatures** (the same temperature as the surrounding air or the room they are in).

Non-perishable foods, for example dry cereals, sugar, dried beans and flour, have very long shelf-lives and are stored at ambient temperatures, away from dampness. Canned foods, UHT (ultra heat treated, long life) products such as milk and fruit juices also have long shelf-lives *until they are opened*, then they become very perishable. Frozen foods and vacuum-sealed products also become perishable once they are thawed or opened.

These foods are perishable and must be chilled or frozen.

These foods are semi-perishable and can be stored at room temperature.

These foods are non-perishable and each has a long shelf-life, for example 3 months for the flour and at least 2 years for the sugar.

The correct temperatures for storing foods

Chilled foods should be stored between –1 °C and 8 °C (ideally below 4 °C).

Frozen foods should ideally be stored at –29 °C, but no higher than –18 °C.

Food manufacturers, retailers, caterers and consumers are *all responsible* for storing food correctly so that it is fit to eat.

Food manufacturers

Food manufacturers are responsible for:

- making sure that their employees work in a clean and hygienic way
- checking the quality of the ingredients they use
- cooking perishable foods thoroughly, then chilling them quickly
- testing a product to check how long a shelf-life it has
- printing a 'best before' or 'use by' date on the label (see p115)
- packaging the product securely to protect it from dirt, damp, light and damage
- storing the product correctly in the warehouse before it is sent out
- delivering the product safely, for example using refrigerated lorries

Perishable foods like milk must be delivered in refrigerated lorries.

Food retailers

Food retailers are responsible for:

- putting perishable and frozen products into chiller cabinets and freezers in the shop as soon as possible after they have been delivered
- storing perishable foods safely, for example raw foods separate from cooked foods
- stock rotation (selling older products before new ones)
- maintaining freezers and chiller cabinets so that they stay at safe temperatures
- taking out-of-date products off the shelves
- storing non-food products, for example washing powders and scented soaps, away from food products
- storing products safely so consumers don't hurt themselves when taking them off the shelves
- storing products correctly so that they do not get damaged by other products or people
- keeping the warehouse, storage and display areas clean and tidy

Consumers and caterers

Consumers and caterers are responsible for:

- taking food purchases home quickly, and putting perishable products into the refrigerator or freezer straight away (the temperature danger zone for perishable food is 10–63 °C, for example a warm car)
- making sure that their refrigerator and freezer are working at a safe temperature (5 °C or less for a refrigerator and –18 °C or colder for a freezer)
- following the manufacturer's and retailer's instructions for storing different foods (these are printed on the label or package)

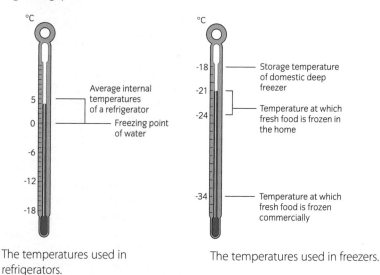

The temperatures used in refrigerators.

The temperatures used in freezers.

- eating or serving foods before the 'use by' and 'best before' dates run out
- storing perishable foods safely, for example, keeping raw and cooked foods separate, preventing raw foods from dripping onto others, removing dirt from salads before refrigerating
- using up older products before new ones

'Best before' and 'use by' dates

'Use by' dates are for perishable foods, which should be used by the date shown, otherwise they may not be safe to eat.

'Best before' dates (day and month) are for less perishable foods. They may also have a number in brackets, for example 17th May (4), which means that four days before the date, the product will be removed from the shelves, but will be safe to eat for another four days.

'Best before end' dates (month and year) are for long-life products, which should be used before the last day of the month shown.

Food manufacturers are required by law to print 'best before' or 'use by' dates on their products.

QUESTIONS

1. What is the difference between perishable and non-perishable foods?
2. Why must perishable foods be stored in cold temperatures?
3. Why must a carton of long-life milk be stored in the refrigerator and used up quickly once opened?
4. Find out why cooked meat must never be stored next to raw meat.
5. Why is it important for shops to rotate their stocks of food?
6. Why is it important for consumers to read food packaging and labels carefully when thinking about storage? What information might they find there?
7. Write down what is wrong with this situation: One morning in July, Sam went to the supermarket and bought some butter, fresh chicken thighs, yogurt, a pack of green salad, two frozen meat pies, and a carton of milk. Afterwards, Sam put the food in the boot of the car, parked it in an open-air car park, and went shopping in town for clothes. Four-and-a-half hours later, after meeting a friend for lunch, Sam drove home and put the food shopping away.

PROJECT Mini-enterprise: starting a small food business

An **enterprise** is a business activity or project. To start a new enterprise, people have to be bold and take a risk. In this case, the enterprise is a small food business, which could, with careful planning and the right target group, be very successful, because food is an essential and enjoyable part of most people's lives and they like to try new products.

Entrepreneurs are people who are prepared to take a risk and start a business. In the food industry, there have been many such people, some of whom started with a small business which, over the years, has become a multinational organisation.

An early Sainsbury's delivery. The first store, which sold butter, milk and eggs, opened in 1869.

Sainsbury's is now a huge, countrywide operation.

There are many things to consider when starting a new food business. It is wise to prepare a detailed **business plan** so that every aspect is covered.

Some of the issues to think about include:

▹ finding suitable premises that you can afford
▹ raising enough money to start and run the business
▹ paying for enough insurance to protect the premises, the staff and members of the public
▹ local laws that limit the number of hours the business can be open every day
▹ objections from local residents
▹ competition from other similar businesses in the area

◗ having enough time to devote to the business when it first starts
◗ finding suitable staff to run the business
◗ meeting all the requirements of the various laws that apply to food businesses

A number of people and organizations set standards and offer advice to people working in the food industry. They include:

◗ **Financial advisers** work out the best way to raise money to start a business and how to invest more money in it once it starts.
◗ **Solicitors and lawyers** advise on buying premises, business law, employing people, and dealing with the public.
◗ **Environmental health officers** advise and check to make sure that the food business is run hygienically and safely, and does not become a nuisance to people who live nearby (for example, because of smells, noise or rubbish).
◗ **Trading standards officers** make sure that the food business is run within the law and that customers are treated fairly.

There are many different **laws** that food businesses must obey. These laws are concerned with the following issues:

Health and safety at work Employers and employees are both responsible for making sure that the workplace is healthy and safe for them to work in and for the public to visit and use. They have to do this by:

◗ identifying risks and hazards and removing or reducing them to prevent accidents or health risks
◗ training the staff to identify and report hazards
◗ training the staff to deal with accidents and emergencies
◗ training the staff to handle and use equipment properly and safely
◗ providing the staff and the public with proper facilities, for example good lighting, sufficient ventilation and warmth, washing facilities and drinking water, enough space, and clearly marked and unobstructed exits from the premises

Food safety (see p34) Every year thousands of people suffer from food poisoning, and some die because of it. Employers and employees must try to prevent this by:

◗ keeping themselves and their workplace, equipment and premises clean and hygienic
◗ identifying risks by carrying out a HACCP (see p36)
◗ preventing food from being contaminated by vermin, insects, dirt, other foods, chemicals and germs
◗ buying, storing, preparing, cooking and serving food in a hygienic and safe way

PROJECT

Industrial relations For a business to be successful, there needs to be a good relationship and cooperation between employers and their employees. This can be achieved by:

▶ good communication, so that everyone knows what is expected of them and what to do if there is a problem

▶ providing equal opportunities, pay and responsibilities where possible, for all groups of people

▶ providing a good working environment that is fair, efficient and happy, and rewards success

Good communication between employees with different responsibilities is essential to the success of any food business.

Brief

In a group of four to six people, form a small food business that fits one of these categories:

• **providing a service**, for example fast food, snack meals, packed or light lunches, party food, drinks, picnic hampers

• **inventing a new product**, for example a new type of bread, soup, drink, snack, ice-cream, biscuit

• **improving an existing product**, for example a curry, pasta meal, vegetarian meal, a product for a special diet, packaging for disabled people, labelling of food products

Research

❖ Decide which type of product or service you want to provide.

❖ Identify your target group.

❖ Research and identify the lifestyle of your target group.

❖ Carry out market research to find out what people want and how many people want or need your product or service.

❖ Decide how you will raise the money to set up your business.

❖ Decide how you will price your product or service so that you will be able to pay back any borrowed money and make a profit.

❖ Decide how you will market (advertise and promote) your

product or service so that you will reach and interest as many people as possible: for example, you could use ICT to produce leaflets, catalogues, business cards, flyers (leaflets put inside newspapers and magazines or put through letter-boxes), posters, video or audio advertisements.

❖ For a product, decide on its size, shape, colour, flavour, packaging and labelling.

❖ Design a system for manufacturing the product in high volume, to a high quality, in an efficient way.

❖ For a service, decide on a logo, equipment required, who does which job, and how you will deal with jobs such as buying ingredients, dealing with orders, disposing of rubbish and clearing up.

What to produce

▶ a specification for your product or service

▶ a sample (prototype) of your product or a leaflet explaining your service (with an order form if appropriate)

▶ a folder explaining all about your business, including how, as a group, you have planned, designed, organized and promoted the business.

If you have a special exhibition day for your mini-enterprise, you will need to do the following:

▶ Prepare a stall or stand to display your product or service. To attract people to your display make sure it is:

  ▶ clearly labelled so people know who you are and what you are offering

  ▶ colourful and interesting (use balloons, posters, badges, table decorations, lights, streamers, etc)

  ▶ neatly and clearly set out in a sensible order

▶ Promote your business on the day, with leaflets, special offers (for example buy two get one free, 10% off for the first 10 customers, get a free badge or balloon with each product), and small samples to taste.

▶ Be prepared to answer questions about your business, and have information available for people to read.

▶ Make sure that all the people in your group are wearing clean clothes or aprons and have clean hands and nails (you could all wear the same colour apron, badge or hat to give your business a unique image).

▶ Have suitable equipment ready for serving the food hygienically and conveniently, for example tongs and plastic gloves, serviettes, plastic or paper bags, disposable cups (insulated for hot liquids), plastic disposable spoons.

PROJECT   Bread batch production

There are many different types of bread products available to buy, some of which are based on recipes from other countries.

Leavened bread is the name given to bread that has been made to rise by **yeast**, which is a microscopic plant that turns sugars into carbon dioxide gas and alcohol. The gas makes the bread dough rise and gives it a light texture. Farmhouse and bloomer white loaves, ciabatta, granary, French bread and wholemeal bread are all made using yeast. **Unleavened** bread is not risen, and has a denser texture. Examples of unleavened bread include tortillas, matzos, oatcakes and crisp breads.

Most bread is made using wheat flour, but other cereals, for example rye and barley, can also be used. Apart from the basic ingredients of flour, water, salt and yeast, other ingredients can be added to breads, including

- dried fruits
- onions and garlic
- herbs and spices
- olive or other oil
- seeds, for example poppy, sesame, pumpkin, sunflower
- dried tomatoes
- cheese
- cooked meats, for example salami, ham

These days, bread is available in a variety of shapes and sizes, and is not always made from the traditional wheat flour.

Bread products baked in a commercial bakery are made in volume, and should all be the same size and shape.

Brief

Design and make a new bread roll or small loaf product, to appeal to young people. The product is to be made in volume, as it would be in a commercial bakery. Each product should be the same as the others in the batch.

Research

* Identify the target group.
* Identify what appeals/does not appeal to them about bread products.
* Find out how commercial bakeries produce bread products in volume (your local supermarket in-store bakery might be willing to arrange for your class to visit).
* Identify the manufacturing processes that are used to make bread products.
* Find out what type of packaging is best for bread products.
* Identify the critical control points in the manufacturing process for bread products.

Your specification

▶ Design a specification for your product.
▶ Identify how you will build quality assurance into your design.
▶ Identify how your product will be made in volume, for example how will you ensure that each product is the same weight, size, shape, colour, texture?
▶ Prepare a hazard analysis (see p36) for your product.
▶ Prepare a prototype and a batch of your product
▶ Evaluate the production of your product – could any improvements be made to any of the ingredients or processes? Identify how your product would be marketed, packaged and priced.

Unit 11 — Using ICT to link with the world outside school

Working in a group or team

By the end of this section, you should be able to:
- Identify ways in which ICT can enable you to work in a team to produce a project.
- Identify ways in which ICT can enable you to work in a team with people in other organizations and countries.

It is very common for several people to work together on a project, as a team. The team will be made up of people with different skills and expertise, which they use to complete different parts of the project. Sometimes, people from other organizations or countries may be asked to help with the project, for example as an adviser, or to try out a product and evaluate it.

Designing and developing a new food product

To design and develop a new food product, the following groups of people might be involved:

A **project coordinator/team leader** to organize other people, delegate (give out) tasks, and bring the whole project together once it is finished.

Market researchers to find out what people want and like.
Product designers to design and develop the new product.
Marketing and advertising experts to promote the new product.
Food technologists to make a new product to the design specification and test it to see that it is safe, suitable and stable.
Home economists to make the new product and develop recipes using it and other ingredients to encourage consumers to use it.
A **food photographer** to photograph the product for advertisements.
Food packaging experts to design and develop suitable packaging.
Nutrition experts to advise about the food value of the product.
Farmers/growers to advise about cost, growing conditions, harvesting and storage.

Food photographers are skilled at photographing food so that it looks as appetizing as possible.

To search the Internet, open a search engine and enter one or more key words, then choose from the list of websites containing those words. To narrow your search, try to make your key words as specific as possible.

ICT and teamwork

ICT has transformed the way in which people communicate and work with each other:

▶ The Internet enables people to find out information on a huge variety of subjects from all over the world, in a matter of seconds.

▶ E-mail is a fast way of sending a message to someone and receiving a reply.

▶ Pages of information (words and pictures) can be sent to someone, as an attachment to an e-mail, and can be downloaded (and printed) by them.

▶ Fax messages, sent via telephone lines, have also made communications much faster.

Using these forms of communication, people can work together, as a team, on a project without actually meeting each other, or can hold a conference where they share ideas, experiences and information. This means that people from different countries can become a team. This is called remote conferencing.

Databases

When working on a project, large amounts of information are gathered, including:

▶ contacts (names of people and organizations, telephone numbers, e-mail addresses, etc.)

▶ reports, studies, letters

▶ graphs, tables, charts, pictures

▶ ideas and suggestions

On a computer such information can be stored on a **database**, so that it is all together in a suitable order, and can be accessed (found) very easily and quickly.

QUESTIONS

1 A food manufacturer wants to develop a new organic vegetarian range of foods for babies. As team leader, what team of people would you put together, and what would you ask each of them to do?

2 How did people living in different places communicate with one another before fax machines and the Internet were invented?

3 For people working on a project together, what differences would this have made?

P R O J E C T   ICT activity

Brief

Your local community has an open-air market that for many years has sold fruit, vegetables, cheese, eggs, fish, meat, spices, dried beans, fruits and lentils, flowers, bread, pies and cakes, kitchen and garden equipment and wines. The market is open on Monday, Wednesday, Friday and Saturday, all year round. Most of the fresh food sold in the market is grown and produced locally, and local people think it is good-quality and reasonably priced.

Fresh cheeses are among the many products on offer at open-air markets.

A market is often the best place to find locally grown fresh fruit and vegetables.

A supermarket company plans to build a large store on the outskirts of the town, which will be 6 kilometres away from the market and local shops. There will be bus services between the store and the town.

The market traders are worried about the impact that the store will have on their businesses. They have decided that the only way they can compete is to improve their services, advertise and promote themselves. They plan to:

▶ open every day during the week, including alternate Sunday mornings

▶ encourage local schools to visit some of the local farms that supply the food

▶ start an ordering and delivery service targeted at people without transport, and local community groups, for example luncheon clubs, playgroups

▶ run special events to promote particular foods throughout the year, for example summer fruits and salads, turkeys, winter root vegetables, local cheeses

▶ open a small open-air café selling hot and cold drinks, snacks and lunches

They have asked pupils at the local school to be involved in a project to help promote the market, in the following ways:

▶ design and make a range of promotional materials to be distributed to the local community

▶ design and make a range of food products using components bought from the market, and set these out on a promotional stall in the market, local library, and community centre

Don't forget to carry out your research and produce your specifications.

Research

❖ Identify why local markets are a valuable part of the community. Think about things like prices, freshness, local produce, social importance, and their role in the the local economy.

❖ Identify the impact that large supermarkets can have on local communities. Think about things like how people will travel to and from them, pollution, prices, effect on local shops, convenience to shoppers, and using up land.

❖ What often happens to local shops when a large supermarket starts to trade nearby?

❖ Identify ways in which you could use ICT to help collect, use and store information about the project, and make the promotional material.

❖ Identify why local shops and market traders have difficulty competing with large supermarkets.

❖ Identify the types of products that could be made to attract customers to use the market.

❖ Identify the target groups who would most benefit from having a delivery service from the local market.

❖ Identify other ways in which people could be encouraged to use the market.

❖ Use the Internet to find out about markets, farmers' markets, market traders' organisations, and other local groups who have worked together to support their local market.

Unit (12) Moving on to Key Stage 4

By the end of this section, you should be able to:

▸ Apply your knowledge and understanding of food technology to different tasks.
▸ Design products that show that you understand the needs and requirements of other people.
▸ Evaluate and assess what you have learned in Key Stage 3, so that you can progress to Key Stage 4.

In Key Stage 3, you have been learning about the design process and how it is applied to food products. In order to understand how to design and develop new food products, you have also learned about what food is, where it comes from, how it is processed and what happens when it is put with other foods. You have learned about why we need food and what foods do for our health, and what can go wrong if foods are not prepared or stored correctly, or if we eat too much or too little of certain types of food.

Professional food designers have to understand food and people in order to make suitable and successful products. In Key Stage 4, Food Technology enables you to apply what you know and understand about food and people to real situations. You will be able to investigate a design problem in great detail, and produce a solution to the problem in the form of a report and a food product.

The briefs that follow will give you an opportunity to put into practice what you already know about researching a problem and designing a food product to solve it. Go ahead and let your designing skills flow!

Briefs

1. Through market research, a manufacturer has realized that a significant number of single men and women find it difficult to cook, and want a range of complete ready meals that they can easily prepare for themselves. Investigate this and design a suitable range of products.

2. A local home for young adults with physical and learning disabilities is trying to encourage its residents to become more independent by enabling them to prepare some of their meals in small groups. Some of the residents have problems reading and following instructions on the labels, and with opening packaging.

Investigate this problem, and identify ways in which manufacturers could help such customers to use their products more easily.

3. A local church wants to open a senior citizens' luncheon club, in which volunteers will prepare, cook and serve a two-course hot meal to 60 senior citizens, once a week. The church has a good-sized kitchen and hall. You have been asked to advise and help them set up the club, and design a range of menus that will be used throughout the year, on a rotation basis.

Identify all the different issues that the club will have to consider, and which outside agencies they will have to inform about the running of the club.

4. A take-away pizza company wants to set up an Internet-based ordering service, and has asked you to design a web page and order form. Investigate what information you would need to include on the web page and order form, and how the company would process the orders and receive payment from customers.

Identify the potential problems and benefits of such a system, for both the customers and the company.

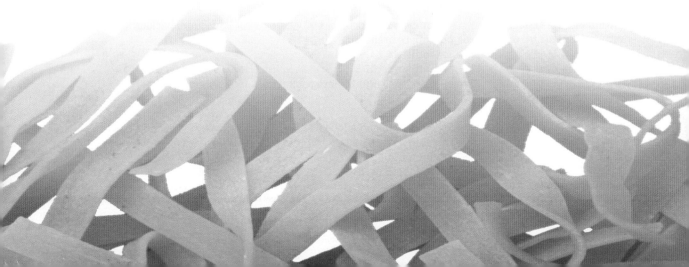

INDEX